Nicholas II

by Marvin Lyons

Edited by Andrew Wheatcroft

Routledge & Kegan Paul London

Nicholas II
The Last Tsar

First published 1974
by Routledge & Kegan Paul Ltd,
Broadway House, 68–74 Carter Lane,
London EC4V 5EL
Printed in Great Britain by
Jarrold & Sons Ltd, Norwich
© Marvin Lyons 1974

ISBN 0 7100 7802 1

To so very many, but most particularly to

E. D. D.

the kindest and dearest of friends, to whom I am indebted beyond measure . . .

Contents

Preface

During the course of research involved in the preparation of a biography of the Emperor Nicholas II of Russia, I became more and more convinced that any definitive work should be heavily illustrated. Over a period of years, large numbers of photographs belonging to individuals connected with or related to the late Emperor or his family were made available for the project. At an early stage in its preparation, I discovered that the coverage provided by the approximately 35,000 photographs available for the project was incomplete. Gaps existed of such a serious nature that completion and publication were out of the question unless they could be filled. This was done and I must state how grateful I am to those who provided such generous assistance to solve what was a serious problem.

Assistance was given not only through the provision of photographs but also with information. I am certain that the reader will appreciate the problem of attempting to identify thousands of old photographs of unknown people, places and events. Unfortunately, all too many of the photographs had no identifying information at all attached to them and there are still many which have not been identified to the degree desired. Those ladies and gentlemen who gave their time and searched their memories to identify their friends and kinsmen and events in their long-lost but still loved world did so out of interest and kindness. They opened doors long closed to provide assistance and, for that alone, there can be no limit to my appreciation.

Editor's note

In a photographic biography, the balance between text and illustrations must always represent an uneasy compromise. In this study the aim has been to cut the text to a minimum, and to allow the photographs to create their own impression. The text aims to introduce a particular group of photographs, rather than provide a continuous narrative accompaniment. Similarly, the selection of photographs is also delicately balanced. Where possible, photographs have been chosen for their visual impact, but historical accuracy has made it vital to include a number of photographs whose quality is poor, but whose value as historical documents is considerable. In particular, many of the photographs taken after Nicholas's abdication were produced and stored under poor conditions and their standard is low.

Two further principles have been implicit in the choice of photographs. Like most monarchs, Nicholas II's public life was photographed exhaustively, as much of the material in this volume indicates. But the Emperor, his family and the Imperial household were passionate amateur photographers, and much survives which counterbalances the formality of State and official occasions with the warmth and friendliness of their family circle. In this book we have tried to indicate both aspects of Nicholas's life.

All dates are given old style, and patronymics have been used only where necessary to avoid confusion, e.g. between Nicholas II and his uncle. Titles have been used selectively, as have the intimate names within the Imperial family.

A. W.

Acknowledgments

I wish to express my sincere gratitude and appreciation to the following ladies and gentlemen who have provided materials or have otherwise been of assistance during the preparation of this book:

General Serge Andolenko(†), Colonel Serge Apuchtin(†), Baroness Anna Benois-Tcherkessoff, Mrs Helen Bezak(†), Miss Helen Bibikov, Countess Mary Bobrinsky, Marie Petrovna von Bock, Mme Tatiana Botkin, AMC, Mrs Marina Bowater, Colonel and Mrs J. J. von Bretzel, Prince Paul Chavchavadze(†), Colonel Peter de Daehn(†), Mr and Mrs Alexander von Daehn, Lieutenant-Colonel Ivan Daragan, Baron Nicholas Dellingshausen(†) and Baroness Dellingshausen, Colonel Serge Dirine(†), Colonel Gabriel Dolenga-Kovalevsky, Mrs Helen Eklof, Colonel Nicholas Galushkin(†), Mr Frederick Gilliard, Mr Paul Goudime, Captain Alexander Gramotine(†), HRH Prince Peter of Greece, Countess Olga Hendrikov, Mr Vladimir Heroys, Countess Marina Heyden, Colonel Dimitri Hodnev, Colonel Alexander Hoerschelmann, Commander Basil Hwoschinsky, Captain Vladimir Kamensky, Professor George Katkov, Count Wladimir Kleinmichel, Mrs Ara de Korostovetz, Count Alexander Koutaissoff, Mr and Mrs Leo Kukuranov, Mr Tihon Kulikovsky, Mrs Wladimir von der Launitz, Captain Alexander Linitsky, Mme A. Lodigensky, Colonel Vladimir de Martinoff, Baron Alexander Meller-Zakomelsky, Baroness Nadejda Meller-Zakomelsky, Colonel M. A. Mikoulinsky(†), Mme Hélène de Monbrison, Lieutenant Michael Moukhanov, Countess Catherine Nieroth, Captain Eugène Nogaetz, Colonel Theo Olferieff(†), Mrs Marjorie Merriweather Post(†), Prince Ivan Poutiatine, Colonel Alexander Romanenko, HSH Prince Wladimir Romanov, Mr Marvin Ross, HH Prince Dimitri of Russia, HH Prince Vsevolod of Russia(†), Mr Roman Sagovsky, Mr and Mrs Dimitri Shvetzoff, Mrs Nina Spiridovitch, Mr Alexander Stacevich, Baron Alexander Stackelberg, Baron Constantine Stackelberg, Prince Nicolas Sviatopolk-Mirsky, Lieutenant-General Michael Swetchine(†), Mrs George Synnerberg, Mr Alexis Tatistcheff, Count Dimitri Tatistcheff(†), Countess Marie Tolstoy(†), Mrs Helen Tolstoy-Miloslavsky, Mrs Helen Torello, Captain Nicholas Touroveroff(†), Commander George Vesselago(†), Mrs Anna Voeikoff, Mr Nicholas Voeikoff, Mr N. N. Vorobiov, Mr Arthur Voyce, Colonel Valery Walter, Lady Wernher, Mrs Michel Wittouck, Prince Felix Youssoupoff(†), Colonel Wladimir Zweguintzow(†), and Mrs Gruber of the Virginia Museum of Fine Arts.

(†) deceased.

I am particularly indebted to HRH Princess Eugénie of Greece, HH Prince Vasili of Russia and Earl Mountbatten of Burma for the freedom I was given to examine the materials in their archives and the assistance they provided in obtaining materials from other sources; to the late Duke Serge von Leuchtenberg for the interest he took in my work and the effort he made to assist me; to Prince Serge Belosselsky, whose ready but unexpected generosity was such a wonderful surprise; and to Countess Marie Kleinmichel, Count Ivan Stenbock-Fermor, Mr Dimitri Shvetzoff and Baron George Taube for their unfailing good humour and willingness to answer all my questions and assist me wherever and whenever it was possible; and to my wife and family, for so many reasons . . .

Nicholas II

On the day traditionally set aside by the Orthodox Church to commemorate the sufferings and tribulations of St Job, 6 May, Nicholas II was born in the Winter Palace in St Petersburg in 1868. To be born on such a day was an ill omen to the superstitious, and misfortune was to dog Nicholas from his earliest years. His uncle died of tuberculosis (as did his brother), his grandfather perished from a terrorist bomb attack, his only son inherited haemophilia, the bleeding sickness, from his mother. He was to launch Russia, unwillingly, on the most destructive war she had ever experienced, and he was to undergo the degradation of abdication and eventual murder, with all his immediate family, in a drab basement in Ekaterinburg. It is scarcely surprising that Nicholas remarked, more than once, on his unfortunate birthday. It was only through his uncle's unexpectedly early death that he even came to the throne.

Nicholas's grandfather, Alexander II, 'liberator of the serfs', had eight children by his first wife. His eldest son, Nicholas Alexandrovich, was destined to follow his father on the throne, and he was carefully prepared for his future role; his younger brother, Alexander, was given no special education or training, and was destined for the active but slightly aimless life of a Grand Duke. In 1864, when Nicholas Alexandrovich was twenty, preparations were made for his engagement to Princess Dagmar of Denmark. Nicholas Alexandrovich visited Copenhagen for the announcement of their betrothal. However, it was clear that he was seriously ill, and he left for an extended tour of southern Europe, where it was hoped that a warmer climate might help him to recover. But the disease (which was to prove to be tuberculosis) progressed and he died in March 1865. On his deathbed he indicated that his brother Alexander should take his place, not only as Tsarevich, but also as Dagmar's husband. On 11 June the engagement of Alexander and Dagmar was announced, and she was baptized into the Orthodox faith under the name of Marie Feodorovna. They were married late the following year in St Petersburg.

Nicholas II was the oldest of six children. A second son, Alexander, was born on 26 May 1869 but he lived less than a year. George was born in 1871, Xenia in 1875, Michael in 1878 and Olga in 1882.

Nicholas was much more fortunate in his family life than most of the Imperial family. His parents had a strong and lasting relationship, unbroken by quarrels, differences of opinion or extra-marital relationships. Alexander was the first Russian Emperor who was a faithful husband. He was a huge, boyish, uncomplicated man who would accept nonsense from no one. She was very small, beautiful and an extremely sociable woman who enjoyed being Empress and who loved her son very deeply. Their bourgeois family life only tended to accentuate this intimate happy relationship.

Life for the young Nicholas began with the steady routine customary for any child of his station. In 1881 it was all changed with the assassination of his grandfather. The horror-stricken family rushed to the Winter Palace and followed through crowded halls a trail of blood to the Emperor's study. He lay, still alive, on a couch but was so badly mutilated that death was inevitable. The sight was one never to be forgotten by those present.

1 *opposite* Mother and son: Marie Feodorovna and the future Emperor Nicholas II, aged two, St Petersburg, 1870.

2 *above* Alexander II and his children, St Petersburg, 1861.
Left to right: Marie, Serge, Vladimir, Alexander (the future
Alexander III), Alexis, Nicholas.

3 *right* Grand Dukes Nicholas Alexandrovich and
Alexander, about 1862. Nicholas wears the uniform of the
Grodno Hussar Guards, of which he was Colonel-in-Chief,
and Alexander that of His Majesty's Hussar Guards.

4-5 *above* The engaged couple, 1864. Grand Duke Nicholas Alexandrovich and Princess Dagmar (Marie Feodorovna).

6 *left* Setting out for a hunt—the party at the main entrance of Fredensborg Palace, 1864. Queen Louise of Denmark and her children Thyra and Valdemar stand in the doorway. The Prince of Wales, wearing plus-fours, stands in the centre of the picture; on his right, in the light-coloured suit and bowler hat, is Grand Duke Nicholas Alexandrovich, and on his left is King Christian IX; next to the King stands Landgrave Wilhelm of Hesse (in the flat cap).

7-8 *below* The engaged couple, 1866. Grand Duke Alexander, later Alexander III, and Princess Dagmar (Marie Feodorovna).

9 *above*   A stereoscopic picture of Grand Duke Nicholas Alexandrovich with Princess Dagmar and her family on the steps at Fredensborg, 1864. King Christian IX and Queen Louise stand at left front. At the rear, left to right: Landgrave Wilhelm of Hesse, Princess Dagmar (blurred), Grand Duke Nicholas Alexandrovich, Crown Prince Frederick of Denmark and the Prince of Wales. The Princess of Wales stands at right centre, in a white dress.

10 *below*   The Russian grandparents, late 1860s. Emperor Alexander II of Russia (1818–81) and Empress Marie Alexandrovna (1824–80), formerly a Princess of Hesse-Darmstadt.

11 *below*   The Danish grandparents, late 1860s. King Christian IX of Denmark (1818–1906) and Queen Louise (1817–98), formerly a Princess of Hesse-Cassel. They were known to the family as 'Apapa' and 'Amama'.

12 *above*   The Emperor of Russia and his family, St Petersburg, 1869. Seated, left to right: Alexander II, Grand Duchess Marie Feodorovna and her year-old son Nicholas (later Nicholas II), Empress Marie Alexandrovna. Standing, left to right: Grand Duke Paul, Grand Duke Serge, Grand Duchess Marie, Grand Duke Alexis, Grand Duke Alexander (later Alexander III), Grand Duke Vladimir.

13 *right*   Mother and son, Copenhagen, autumn 1869.

14 *far right*   The future Emperor Nicholas II (in centre in white shirt and dark cap), surrounded by members of his 'Danish family', Bernstorf, about 1871. Grand Duchess Marie Feodorovna sits at the top of the steps, holding her infant son George. Just in front of her (left to right) are her sisters Thyra and Alexandra, Princess of Wales, who is holding Princess Maud.

22

15 *left* Grand Duchess
Marie Feodorovna with her
sons, Nicholas and George,
about 1875.

16 *right* Nicholas, Xenia,
George and their parents,
about 1878.

23

17 *left* Grand Duchess Marie
Feodorovna with George and Nicholas,
about 1872.

18 *above left* George and Nicholas,
aged five and eight, St Petersburg, 1876.

19 *above right* Nicholas and George
aged thirteen and ten.

20 *left* Alexander II
on his deathbed,
St Petersburg, April 1881.

21 *right* Nicholas in the
uniform of the Ataman
Cossack Guards Regiment,
about 1881.

22 *left* Mother and son, about 1883.

23 *right* The famous window of the private wagon of the King of Denmark, with signatures scratched into the glass by members of the family during the annual visits to Denmark: Bertie—Alex = the Prince and Princess of Wales; Sasha = Emperor Alexander III; Dagmar = Empress Marie Feodorovna; Willy and Olga = King George I and Queen Olga of Greece; Amama = Queen Louise of Denmark; Apapa = King Christian IX of Denmark; Eddy = the Duke of Clarence; Victoria = Princess Victoria of Wales; Fred and Louise = Prince (later King) Frederick of Denmark and Princess Louise; Waldemar = Prince Waldemar of Denmark; Minny = Empress Marie Feodorovna; Tino = Crown Prince (later King) Constantine of Greece; Nicky = the future Nicholas II; George = Grand Duke George of Russia; Georgi = Grand Duke George of Russia; May and Georgie = the future King George V and Queen Mary; Xenia = Grand Duchess Xenia of Russia; Misha = Grand Duke Michael of Russia; Thyra = the Duchess of Cumberland.

24 *below* Nicholas, George and Mr Heath, Copenhagen, 1884. Charles Heath (1826–1900), an English gentleman and graduate of Cambridge, came to Russia before the Crimean War. One of his first positions was that of English tutor to Serge and Paul, the two youngest sons of Emperor Alexander II. After holding professorial positions at the Imperial Alexander Lyceum and the Naval Academy, he was appointed tutor in English to the two eldest sons of the Tsarevich Alexander. From that time (1879) until his death, he remained an intimate of the Imperial family. He became a very close friend of Alexander III and his family: all the Imperial family, except Nicholas II who was then in the Crimea, came to his funeral.

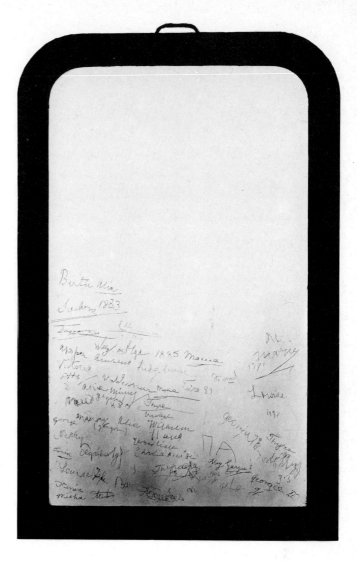

Nicholas. 1884.
For Lala

Georgy November. 1884. For Lala

For dear Tino from Nicky. 1886.

25-6 *above* Nicholas and George, aged sixteen and thirteen. An identical pair of photographs remained in a leather frame on a small table in Alexander III's private study at Gatchina, until it was looted and burnt by the Germans during the Second World War.

27 *left* A photograph sent by Nicholas, wearing the uniform of the Ataman Cossack Guards Regiment, to his cousin Crown Prince Constantine of Greece. One of Alexander III's first acts after coming to the Throne was to order that military costume be simplified and 'Russianized'. The differences between this and the uniform worn at the beginning of the reign (see no. **21**) are obvious.

28 George and Nicholas, aged fifteen and eighteen, at Livadia, 1886. From infancy until George's illness forced his 'exile' to the Caucasus, Nicholas and his brother were almost never separated. They shared the same bedroom, the same tutors, the same friends and amusements. They were as close as brothers could be.

On 23 June 1887 Nicholas began his military service. Although the army had been a daily and intimate part of his life from early youth, and although he held numerous honorary ranks and appointments, it was only then that he put on the uniform and epaulettes of a serving officer. It was the most important and formative event of his life. The legacy of his military service would remain—a deep yearning to return to that pleasant and carefree life of the young officer. He wrote cheerfully to his mother:

> I am now happier than I can say to have joined the army and every day I become more and more used to camp life. Every day we drill twice—either there is target practice in the morning and battalion drill in the evening or the other way round . . . I am quite used to this now and already it seems to me that months have passed since I joined my regiment . . . We have lunch at 12.00 and dine at 8, with siesta and tea in between. The dinners are very merry; they feed us well. After meals, the officers practise hard on the giant stride or play billiards, skittles, cards, or dominoes. I always play skittles and we have some very good games in spite of the poor condition of the skittle alley.

Lunch

29-31 No. **30** (centre) left to right: Crown Prince Constantine of Greece, Grand Duchess Elisabeth, Grand Duke Alexander Mikhailovich, Nicholas, George, Grand Duke Serge Mikhailovich.

Emperor Alexander III was concerned about the possibility of morally corrupting influences being brought to bear on the heir during his period in camp. As he had rather a poor opinion of officers, the strictest possible instructions about their behaviour were given to the senior officers of the Guards.

As a Second Lieutenant with the 1st 'His Majesty's' Company of the Preobrajensky Regiment, Nicholas was frequently visited by his parents, cousins, brother and Mr Heath. His uncle, Serge Alexandrovich commanded the regiment and his cousins Alexander and Serge Mikhailovich were also serving as subaltern officers. At least a dozen other members of the family were similarly employed with the Guards that summer in the camp at Krasnoe Selo and the surrounding villages.

The following group of photographs were taken on three separate occasions during that seven-week period.

On the giant stride

Above, left to right

32 Nicholas, Princess Alexandra of Greece, Grand Duchess Elisabeth, Crown Prince Constantine of Greece.

33 Princess Alexandra, Grand Duke Alexander Mikhailovich, Nicholas, Grand Duke Serge Mikhailovich and Grand Duchess Elisabeth.

34 Grand Duke Serge, Princess Alexandra, Grand Duke George and Prince George of Greece.

35 Nicholas stands apart on the left, next to Crown Prince Constantine with Grand Duke Cyril on his shoulders, Grand Duke George with Grand Duke Boris on his shoulders.

Below, left and right

36-7 Overlooking part of the camp at Krasnoe Selo. In no. **36** Nicholas is giving his cousin, Crown Prince Constantine, a cigarette. In no. **37** the cousins have switched caps.

On 11 August 1887, at the conclusion of the manœuvres, the Emperor and his family sailed for Denmark, accompanied by Queen Olga and Crown Prince Constantine of Greece. The yacht, as far as can be determined from the photographs, was the *Tsarevna*; it was much smaller than the later yachts *Polar Star* and *Standart*.

38 Emperor Alexander III with two ladies of the household.

39 *above left* Queen Olga of Greece, George, Alexander III, Crown Prince Constantine of Greece, Empress Marie Feodorovna (holding Olga), Nicholas, Xenia; Michael sits in front.

40 *above right* Crown Prince Constantine escorts his aunt (Empress Marie Feodorovna) for a walk around the deck.

41 *right* Two sisters: the Princess of Wales and the Empress of Russia.

42 *above*   On the steps of Fredensborg Palace, September 1887. Nicholas is seated on the steps in the centre of the picture. Twelve of those present were either ruling monarchs, or would become so.

43 *above* The family meets again, on a less pleasant day, on approximately the same spot. Nicholas stands next to Crown Prince Constantine beside the lamp.

44 *right* Nicholas and Xenia, almost certainly in Denmark in 1887. All the children of Alexander III had happy, affectionate natures, and the relationship between Nicholas and his sister was particularly close.

45 *left* Dinner at Fredensborg, about 1889.

46 *below* The family on holiday in Denmark, 1889.

Чєрноморєцъ. Venice.
1889.

47 *right*   Aboard the *Chernomorets* (*Black Sea*) at Venice, October 1889. Nicholas was on his way to Athens for the wedding of his cousin Crown Prince Constantine of Greece to Princess Sophie of Prussia.

48 Emperor Alexander III, the Princess of Wales and Empress Marie Feodorovna in Denmark, about 1890.

Nicholas's military service was intended as a form of education, designed to familiarize him with the main branches of the Russian army. In 1887 and 1888 he served first as a subaltern officer and then as a company commander in an infantry regiment—the Preobrajensky. In 1889 and 1890 this process was continued—with service first as a subaltern officer and then squadron commander in His Majesty's Hussar Guards. Familiarity with the third branch came as a result of his service in 1891 and 1892 as commander of the 1st Section of the 1st Battery of the Guards Horse Artillery.

All Russia's Emperors in the nineteenth century saw active service as regimental officers as part of their education, and both Alexander II and Alexander III had served in the Preobrajensky and the Hussars. The difference was that for Nicholas it was a much more agreeable and profound experience. He always looked back with yearning and affection to those years filled with physical activity, good fellowship, to the possibility of obtaining immediate and visible results upon issuing a command, and to freedom from great responsibilities.

49 *below*   The young Hussar, 1890.

50 *below*   Nicholas's house in Russkoe Koporskoe.

51 *below* In camp at Russkoe Koporskoe, July 1890. Nicholas is fifth from left.

52 *above* Officers of the 1st Squadron of His Majesty's Guards Regiment, 1890. Left to right: Alexander Constantinovich von Meier, Ivan Nikolaevich Svechin, Sergei Sergeevich Golovin, Nicholas, Prince Lev Ivanovich Dondukov-Izedinov.

53-4 *left*   Nicholas serving as a section commander with the Guards Horse Artillery near Krasnoe Selo, 1892.

55 *below*   On 1 January 1893 Nicholas was promoted to Colonel and commander of the 1st Battalion of the Preobrajensky Regiment. He is seen here with his officers.

56 Nicholas and some of his comrades of the Preobrajensky Regiment outside the Regimental Officers' Club in the summer camp of the Imperial Guard at Krasnoe Selo. Left to right: Dzhunkovski, unidentified officer, Prince Peter of Oldenburg, Duke George of Leuchtenburg (of the Horse Guards Regiment), Duke Nicholas of Leuchtenburg, Mikhailov, Nicholas, Count Loris–Melikov, Paton.

Most of Russia's Empresses and Grand Duchesses by marriage were German and, as more than one wit has pointed out, the amount of Russian blood in the last Romanovs was comparable with the drop of wine in a glass of water.

Hesse-Darmstadt had already provided one Empress of Russia (Empress Marie Alexandrovna, consort of Alexander II), and had only missed providing another by the untimely death of the first wife of Grand Duke Paul Petrovich, later Emperor Paul I, in 1776. In June 1884 this relationship was strengthened with the marriage of Nicholas's uncle, Grand Duke Serge, to the beautiful Princess Elisabeth (Ella) of Hesse, daughter of the British Princess Alice (who died in 1878) and Grand Duke Louis IV.

This marriage opened a line of communication for Nicholas with his uncle's new sister-in-law Princess Alix of Hesse. Although he saw her only a few times between 1884 and 1893, Nicholas was attracted to her and he was not easily deflected.

57 A family group at Darmstadt, June 1888.

58 *above* The four daughters of Grand Duke Louis IV of Hesse and the Rhine, April 1885. Left to right: Irene (later Princess Henry of Prussia), Victoria (later Princess Louis of Battenberg), Elisabeth (Grand Duchess Serge of Russia), Alix (later Empress Alexandra of Russia).

59 *right* The house-party at Ilinskoe, the estate of Grand Duke Serge Alexandrovich near Moscow, during the visit of the Grand Duchess Elisabeth Feodorovna's family, September 1890. Princess Alix of Hesse-Darmstadt sits arm in arm with the bearded Grand Duke Serge in the centre of the picture.

In late 1890 Nicholas, his brother George and his cousin Prince George of Greece set out on a major trip to the Fast East on board a Russian warship, the *Pamiat Azova*, accompanied by an entourage of young noblemen under the command of Major-General Prince Vladimir Bariatinski. The trip was to take them from Greece to Egypt, India, Ceylon, Siam, Singapore, Japan and on to Vladivostok, from where the party was to make its way overland back to St Petersburg.

Prince Bariatinski was an intimate friend of Alexander III, and his son Anatole was Nicholas's childhood friend and playmate; the trip was to be recorded by Prince Ukhtomsky, the only member of the party who was not a member of the Imperial household. Of the others, Volkov had been Nicholas's squadron commander in the Hussars, Prince Obolensky and Prince Kochubei occupied important positions at Court, and the careers of all three were to be fostered and enhanced by the patronage of their young travelling companion.

The trip was interesting, but it was marred by the discovery on the way to India that Grand Duke George was ill (it was established later that he had tuberculosis). He was immediately sent home and spent most of his remaining years at Abas Tuman in the Caucasus.

The visit to Siam was especially enjoyable and was the start of a lasting friendship between the two ruling families. Princes of the Siamese Royal Family were sent to be educated in the Corps of Pages and two of them served as officers in the Russian Imperial Guard.

60 The barge carrying Nicholas and his companions comes alongside the *Pamiat Azova* in which they will be travelling.

61 While the *Pamiat Azova* anchored at Port Said for a two-week stay in November 1890, the party enjoyed the hospitality of the Khedive in Cairo. However, they spent most of their time visiting the monuments and ruins of ancient Egypt. At the Pyramids they were joined by the Crown Prince of Sweden and his party, who were also visiting Egypt.

The only unpleasant event of the trip occurred in Japan when a Japanese policeman attacked Nicholas with his sword and attempted to kill him. Fortunately, two Japanese rickshaw men and Prince George of Greece intervened and he received only one blow on the forehead. Nicholas wished to ignore the entire affair as he was not seriously injured, although he had occasional headaches as a result for the rest of his life. Marie Feodorovna's letter to her son reflects the horror with which the news of the attack was received by his parents, and their subsequent relief:

> God be praised! No words can tell what dread and sorrowing tears we received that *terrifying* news with! I could not believe my eyes and thought I must be going mad! How lucky your telegram telling us you were safe came first, in fact in the morning just when I was getting up—Bariatinsky's telegrams with details only arrived at three in the afternoon. You can well imagine what *agonies* we suffered waiting for that telegram all through the day! It was more than terrible. We kept getting other most upsetting telegrams from Japan, which said you had received 2 sabre cuts on the head, that you were *seriously* wounded, but there was hope the wound was not dangerous! It was indeed more than one could stand. Our cup of sorrow was full, and I assure you Papa and I were at the end of our strength . . . I kiss you in my thoughts with all my heart and soul, and congratulate you again and again, my angel Nicky, on your merciful escape.

62 Making use of local transport: Nicholas and Grand Duke George sit on donkeys in the centre of the picture.

63 Before lunch at the Pyramids, 13 November. Nicholas, in a light suit and bowler hat and holding a walking-stick, strikes a classic pose before the Great Pyramid. His brother George, already beginning to show signs of tuberculosis, looks over his left shoulder. The Crown Prince of Sweden stands on Nicholas's right. The Khedive Tewfik Pasha, their host, stands a little in front of the others.

64 While waiting for lunch to be served, Nicholas, Grand Duke George and Prince George of Greece pose with opium pipes in the Temple of Amon at Karnak, 17 November.

65 Moving in procession through Benares, the elephants and their passengers stop to be photographed. On the first elephant, Nicholas and the Maharaja; on the second, Prince George of Greece and the Maharaja's heir.

66 King Chulalongkorn of Siam with his guests and their respective entourages, Bangkok, 1891. Nicholas is wearing the uniform of His Majesty's Hussar Guards.

67 *above*   Nicholas in a Japanese rickshaw just before the attack on his life in Otsu; Nagasaki, April 1891.

68 *right*   The scene of the street in Otsu immediately after the attack by the Japanese policeman, Otsu, 30 April 1891.

To my beloved Georgie

his ever thankful Nicky

69 *above* A photograph given to Prince George of Greece by Nicholas shortly after the attack on his life.

70 May 1893 was the Golden Wedding of Apapa and Amama, the King and Queen of Denmark. For the occasion a particularly large number of members of the family gathered. It was to be the last time they were all together. Alexander III's illness prevented the Russian family from coming in 1894 (he died soon after). Grand Duke George's illness prevented him from coming again. Fredensborg, 1893.

71 A less formal group in Denmark, 1893.

72 Nicholas in the uniform of a Russian naval officer, 1893.

73 Nicholas in England in July 1893 for the wedding of his cousin the Duke of York, later King George V, to Princess Mary (May) of Teck, 6 July 1893. He was delighted at the warmth of his welcome: Edward VII's reaction was predictable. As he wrote to his mother: 'Uncle Bertie [Edward VII] is in very good spirits and very friendly—almost too much so. He, of course, sent me at once a tailor, a bootmaker, and a hatter.'

On 2 April 1894 Nicholas left Gatchina with his uncles Grand Dukes Vladimir, Serge and Paul for the wedding in Coburg of his cousin Princess Victoria of Saxe-Coburg-Gotha to Grand Duke Ernst Ludwig of Hesse and the Rhine, Alix's brother. These family weddings frequently resulted in romances and engagements among the guests; this one would follow the pattern.

Nicholas's attachment to Princess Alix of Hesse did not weaken in the years after their first meeting in 1884. His father strongly opposed the marriage when it was first proposed in 1891, and other matches were suggested. All fell through on the crucial issue of religion, and it was on this ground that his courtship of Alix nearly foundered. But Alexander III's health was declining in 1894, and he agreed that Nicholas should go to Darmstadt to propose to Alix. To gain permission from his parents was one thing, being accepted by his prospective bride was another. Princess Alix was sincerely devoted to her religious beliefs and the idea of changing her faith in order to marry seemed the worst sort of hypocrisy. However, after long talks with Grand Duchess Marie Pavlovna and the Kaiser (who reassured her about the religious differences), she finally consented on the morning of 8 April. For Nicholas it had been a hard struggle, as he revealed to his mother:

> This is how, with God's merciful help, my quest, which seemed so desperate, found its fulfilment. The day after I came here I had a long and very difficult talk with Alix, in which I tried to explain to her that there was no other way for her than to give her consent, and that she simply could not withhold it. She cried the whole time and only whispered now and then 'No, I cannot!' Still I went on, repeating and insisting on what I had said before. And though this talk went on for two hours, it came to nothing because neither she nor I would give in. The next morning we talked in a much calmer way . . .

When, later, she did consent, 'I cried like a child and she did too; but her expression had changed; her face was lit by a quiet content'.

Nicholas spent twelve more days in Germany with his fiancée, travelling about the countryside, visiting relatives and the home of Princess Alix at Darmstadt. It was a period of great happiness and one that they would always recall with pleasure.

74 Nicholas and Alix on the day of their engagement at Rosenau, 8 April 1894.

75 *below* The newly engaged couple
out for a ride in Coburg, April 1894.

76-8 *above, left, centre and right* The engaged couple, Coburg, April 1894.

In the early summer of 1894 Alexander III's health began to give cause for concern. After the wedding of his daughter Xenia to Grand Duke Alexander Mikhailovich at the end of July, it became obvious to all that he was very ill. The doctors were consulted and advised a complete change of scene and a long rest. It was agreed that the trip to Denmark must be cancelled and that the Emperor would go instead to Bielovezh in Poland immediately after the annual visit to the Guard at Krasnoe Selo.

In Poland, however, Alexander's health deteriorated still further. He suffered from insomnia and worried constantly about his son George—whom the Empress had unwisely called back from the Caucasus. It was equally obvious that George, too, was suffering from a progressive (and ultimately fatal) illness.

After two weeks at Bielovezh the Emperor and his family moved to Spala, hoping that the change in environment might somehow improve the Emperor's health and restore his spirits. It did neither and it was announced on 17 September that the Emperor's condition

79 *left*   Alexander III and his youngest son Michael in June 1894.

80 *right*   The ailing Emperor and his entourage, Bielovezh, late August 1894. Sitting on the ground, from left to right: Grand Duke George, Nicholas, Prince Nicholas of Greece, Grand Duchess Olga, Grand Duke Michael. Alexander III is seated behind Grand Duchess Olga.

demanded a warmer climate and that he was leaving for Livadia. The bulletin did not mention that plans had been made for him to go to Corfu.

After three and a half days on the train, the party arrived in Sevastopol and immediately boarded the cruiser *Orel* for the voyage to Yalta. Any trip to Corfu was postponed indefinitely, as Alexander's health would no longer permit the journey. For the next month the Emperor's condition fluctuated and to ease the monotony and take his mind off his health, trips to Yalta and to Massandra were arranged but he returned weakened after a few hours. His future daughter-in-law, Princess Alix of Hesse, was sent for but no one thought to make arrangements for her reception and she travelled across Russia in a public carriage. The rest of the family, too, were summoned, as was the priest Father John of Kronstadt. The decline continued and he died with his wife by his side on the afternoon of 20 October, sitting in a chair in a second-floor room of the Small Palace at Livadia.

81 *above* The Small Palace, Livadia. Emperor Alexander III died on the second floor, in the corner room facing the camera.

82 *below* The arrival of Princess Alix of Hesse-Darmstadt in Alushta, 10 October 1894. With her in the carriage is Nicholas; her sister, Grand Duchess Elisabeth, is standing in the gateway in front of the saluting officer.

83 *right* Thursday 20 October 1894, 2.15 p.m. A sketch from memory by the Court artist M. Zichy of the moment of death.

84-5 The new Emperor, late 1894, in the service uniform of the Guards Horse Artillery. These appear to be from the series of eight studies made by Levitski for the use of the Imperial Mint on coins and medals. Nicholas disliked his profile, finding it too much like that of the murdered Emperor Paul; no other photograph posed in profile is believed to exist.

The marriage of the new Emperor took place in St Petersburg less than four weeks after the death of his father. It was generally agreed that the wedding should be celebrated as soon as possible, and Court mourning was officially lifted for the day. The Dowager Empress was dressed in white and went herself to fetch the bride from her sister's palace on the Nevsky. The Emperor and his brother drove together through the streets without an escort and the only soldiers and policemen to be seen were spectators.

The bride and groom returned to the Anichkov Palace to go on living in Nicholas's cramped apartments until their own residence could be made ready. They had selected the Alexander Palace in Tsarskoe Selo, where his parents had lived for a time. Whether they had consciously decided to abandon St Petersburg as a residence is not certain, but from the time they moved to Tsarskoe in 1895 they rarely spent a night in the capital.

86 *above*   The Emperor and Grand Duke Michael leave for the wedding ceremony.

87 *below*   The Dowager Empress Marie Feodorovna leaves the Anichkov Palace to escort Alix to her wedding.

71

Nicholas II came to the Throne in 1894 an autocrat and believing fully in autocracy. On his sixteenth birthday, when he officially came of age, he took part in a great ceremony before his entire family and the Court during which he swore an oath of allegiance to the Emperor, part of which required him to guard and defend the rights and privileges pertaining to the autocracy of the reigning Emperor. The other male members of the Imperial family took similar oaths. He never took an oath, as some historians have stated, to preserve the autocracy and hand it down intact to his heir, but he most certainly believed that to be his duty.

The ceremonies in Moscow lasted almost a month, from the unannounced arrival of the Imperial couple on 6 May (when they immediately moved into the Petrovsky Palace on the north-west boundaries of the city for three days of prayer), until they went for a rest on 30 May to Ilinskoe, the estate of Grand Duke Serge on the Moscow River outside the city.

After the State entry into the city on 9 May, the Emperor and Empress again retired into seclusion to pray and prepare themselves for the Coronation, which took place on 14 May. It is perhaps fitting that the last event of its kind in Russia should be the first historic event recorded on motion-picture film. The rest of the month was taken up with great reviews, church parades, balls, public events of all kinds—marred only once when a number of people were crushed to death while gifts were being given out on the Khodinski Field.

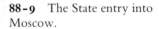

88-9 The State entry into Moscow.

90 *right* The Coronation, 14 May 1896. The ceremony has just ended, and the newly crowned Emperor and his consort have left the cathedral to walk in procession around the Kremlin. The members of the Imperial family and the foreign guests follow. The Russian Grand Duchesses are escorted by foreign Princes, and the first two coming towards the camera are the Emperor's sisters Xenia and Olga.

91 *below* Surrounded by high officials of Church and State and the officers of the Imperial Suite in their round white fur caps, Nicholas passes through the lines of Cuirassiers to be presented to the few of his subjects who were able to crowd into the Kremlin for the occasion.

92 *right* Moving along the Kremlin parade-ground, the procession passes through lines of Hussars from the Emperor's old regiment. The soldiers outside the fence are part of the composite infantry and cavalry regiments formed from the Imperial Guard and sent to Moscow for the Coronation. The temporary huts in the background were erected to house workmen engaged in building a huge monument to Emperor Alexander II.

93 *above*   The Emperor and Empress leaving church after the church parade and service on the Khodinski Field in Moscow, 21 May 1896.

94 *right*   The house-party at Ilinskoe, the estate of Grand Duke Serge Alexandrovich near Moscow, June 1896. Princess Marie of Romania is seated second from left, and on her left is Princess Victoria of Battenberg. Thereafter, Princess Beatrice of Saxe-Coburg-Gotha, the Empress (holding Grand Duchess Olga on her lap), the Duchess of Saxe-Coburg-Gotha, Grand Duke Dimitri Pavlovich, Grand Duchess Elisabeth Feodorovna, and Grand Duchess Victoria of Hesse (holding her son). The Emperor sits in the centre, on the ground.

After the Coronation the Emperor and Empress began a very heavy round of engagements which began with the centenary of the birth of Nicholas I and the ceremonies before his statue in St Petersburg on 25 June. In July they visited Nijni Novgorod Fair and in August their visit to the Imperial Guard camp at Krasnoe Selo was followed by State visits to Vienna and Breslau and the annual journey to Denmark. From Denmark they went to France for a week-long State visit. Finally at the beginning of October, they went to Balmoral to stay with Queen Victoria and then stopped in Darmstadt to see the Empress's brother.

95 With President Faure at Versailles, 1896. Note the Emperor's Cossack and the Empress's Court-Cossack. Nicholas described the scene to his mother: 'We went to Versailles . . . with Faure in a *post chaise à la française* all the way to Versailles—nearly 12 miles—the road was lined with crowds just as in the streets in Paris; my hand got quite numb from so much saluting.'

96 Bernstorf, September 1896. Standing, left to right: Princess of Wales, Prince Waldemar, the Dowager Empress Marie Feodorovna, Nicholas, Queen Louise of Denmark and Princess Victoria of Wales; the Empress sits in front, holding Grand Duchess Olga, with King Christian of Denmark.

97 *above* Nicholas with his firstborn (Grand Duchess
Olga) in 1896.

98 *above* The Emperor and Empress with Grand Duchess
Olga, 1896.

99 *above* At Alexandria-Peterhof, 1898. Left to right: the Mistress of the Court, Princess A. A. Obolensky-Neledinsky-Meletsky; Minister of War, General A. N. Kuropatkin; unidentified Court official; Grand Duchess Olga Alexandrovna; the Minister of Foreign Affairs, Count M. N. Murav'ev; Nicholas; the Commander of the Cossack Escort, Major-General Baron A. E. Meyendorff (saluting).

100 *right* Nicholas and Alix aboard the yacht *Standart* at Sevastopol, 1898.

101 *left* Leaving Copenhagen, 1899. The Emperor turns to shake hands with his cousin Crown Prince Frederick, who is in Russian admiral's uniform. Standing between them in Russian Court uniform is the Russian Foreign Minister, Count M. N. Murav'ev.

102 *below left* The Russian Court's first motor car, at Krasnoe Selo in 1900. The Emperor's old and intimate friend and later the Chief of his Campaign Chancellery, Prince V. N. Orlov, would allow no one else to drive his master. This situation existed for a number of years until his growing girth made it impossible. Grand Duchess Marie Pavlovna appears just to the right of Orlov. Grand Duke Vladimir, Grand Duke Michael, Grand Duchess Olga and the Minister of the Court, Baron Freedericksz, wait for the car to leave.

103 *below* The Emperor and Empress with their households and the Minister of War during the visit of the Emperor's sister, Princess Henry of Prussia, to Livadia in 1901. The Empress is seated third from the left, with Nicholas behind her and her sister next to her. Sitting on the ground, in a white cap, is Count D. F. Heyden. A childhood friend of Nicholas, he succeeded Mamontov (seated at left) as Chief of the Campaign Chancellery. In 1906 he divorced his wife to marry a maid of honour, Olenina (standing). Although divorce was by then not unusual in Russian society, such behaviour was not permitted at Court. Even the friendship of the Emperor could not mitigate Heyden's disgrace and exile.

104 The Emperor in his wife's sitting-room at Alexandria-Peterhof about the turn of the century. The exact date and the identity of the lady, apparently one of the Empress's household, are unknown.

105   The Emperor in his study at Alexandria-Peterhof.

The Imperial family had two private retreats where they could effectively get away from the normal care and restraint of daily life—at Livadia in the Crimea and on the yacht *Standart*. If, on occasion, a part of the family's normal role did intrude in Livadia, it never did on the *Standart*. The Crimea was a semi-tropical paradise, completely unlike the rest of the Empire. It was beautiful, warm, the scent of a hundred different flowers hung in the air; but there were occasional intrusions. The *Standart*, on the other hand, cruising or anchoring in some sheltered cove, was completely isolated from the world. Just one or two of the Emperor's gentlemen, one or two of the Empress's ladies, the officers and crew of the yacht. Here all was peace and amusements were simple—rowing or swimming or picnics on the islands.

Aboard the *Standart*

106 *above* The Emperor and his brother-in-law Prince Louis of Battenberg on the yacht in the Gulf of Finland, August 1901.

107 *above right* The Empress.

108 *right* The Emperor and Empress with their children, 1902. In front, left to right: Marie, Olga and Tatiana.

86

109 *above* Grand Duke Vladimir, at the left, looks on as peasant children present the Emperor and Empress with bread and salt, about 1902. In the background a detachment of firemen are drawn up for inspection.

110–11 *right* Nicholas believed it to be his duty, whenever this was possible, to attend the funerals of officials who had been assassinated. Thus he was present at the funerals in St Petersburg of the assassinated Minister of the Interior, Sipiagin, 4 April 1902 (no. **110**), and that of the Governor-General of the Grand Duchy of Finland, Bobrikov, 8 June 1904 (no. **111**).

112   The arrival of President Loubet of France in Russia at Peterhof, 7 May 1902. The Emperor salutes as the Guard of Honour from the Garde Équipage marches past.

113 The Emperors of Germany and Russia inspect the results of Russian naval gunfire during the visit of the Kaiser to Reval in July 1902. The tall officer to the left of Nicholas is his uncle Grand Duke Alexis Alexandrovich, Commander-in-Chief of the navy.

Military ceremonial dominated the Emperor's official life, from the great set-piece parades, like the May Day review of the Guards in St Petersburg (discontinued after 1904) to the smaller regimental reviews which averaged about one per week during the years of peace. In addition he regularly attended the summer manœuvres at Krasnoe Selo and, less frequently, the large-scale manœuvres held in the provinces. He enjoyed his military duties although his natural shyness often made it difficult, as he wrote to his mother in August 1896:

> The review of August 6 left a very sad impression on me, though everything went off remarkably well. In the morning, before getting into the carriage, I had one of my fits of nerves, which reminded me of the old days when I got them before every review. I felt green and trembled all over. When four battalions and the Artillery had drunk my health, I felt better, and tried to look cheerful, especially when talking to the officers after lunch.

The regimental reviews were usually held in Tsarskoe Selo, Gatchina or Peterhof, or at Krasnoe Selo if the regiment was in camp there. Only rarely were reviews held in St Petersburg; in general, the regiments came to the Emperor, not he to them.

This section is intended to give an impression of the great variety of Nicholas's military duties.

114   The Jubilee of Her Majesty's Lancer Guards Regiment at Peterhof, 16 May 1903; the arrival of the Imperial party, with the Empress at the front talking to Grand Duke Michael Nikolaevich.

115 *above* The Empress with the serving and former officers of her regiment in a formal group taken during the Jubilee celebrations. The Emperor stands next to his wife, also in Lancer uniform.

116 *left* The Emperor and Empress during the 'Te Deum'. This is the only occasion on which the Empress ever appeared on horseback on a formal occasion.

117 *above left*   A review of the Semeonovsky Guards Regiment at Tsarskoe Selo, 21 November 1908.

118 *below left*   A visit to the St Petersburg Guards Regiment in the summer camp of the Imperial Guard at Krasnoe Selo, 16 August 1909. Nicholas is accompanied by his young son Alexei.

119 *above*   During a visit to His Majesty's Hussar Guards Regiment, the Emperor inspected a detachment of Red Cross dogs and their handlers (from the Hussars and the regiments of the 1st Guards Infantry Division). Tsarskoe Selo, 1910.

120 *above* The ground-breaking ceremony for a new church of the 4th 'Imperial Family' Rifle Guards, Tsarskoe Selo, 1912.

121-2 *left and above*   The visit to the 4th 'Imperial Family'
Rifle Guards Regiment for the purpose of inspecting the new
temporary barracks of the newly raised 2nd Battalion at
Tsarskoe Selo, June 1912. After the inspection Nicholas posed
with the officers for the photographer (**122**). This was the
environment in which he felt most at home—among his
officers—and nowhere more so than in the 'Imperial Family'
Rifles.

123 *above* The fête of the Egersky Guards Regiment at Peterhof, 17 August 1912. The Emperor and his son are escorted down the line of soldiers shouting their greeting by the regimental commander, Major-General Iablochkin, and followed by the tall figure of Grand Duke Nicholas Nikolaevich.

124 *right* The review of the Grenadier Guards Regiment in the courtyard of the Catherine Palace at Tsarskoe Selo, 16 April 1913. The officer in the white jacket is the commander of the Imperial Guard, General V. M. Bezobrazov.

Each year the Imperial family would come to Krasnoe Selo to spend a week or so at the camp of the Imperial Guard. When the tradition began is uncertain. Krasnoe had been in use by the army since the middle of the eighteenth century, and the summer quarters of the Imperial Guard since 1819. The house was a small 'palace'; actually a copy of a Swiss chalet built by Empress Alexandra Feodorovna (wife of Emperor Nicholas I) in 1828.

125-6 Escorted by Prince Serge Belosselsky and his brother-in-law Prince Orlov, the young Grand Duchesses watch the manœuvres from the 'Tsar's Mound', an artificial hill from which the Empress and any special guests watched the great parades.

127 *below*   The Emperor talking to his aide-de-camp Colonel M'divani, commander of the 13th 'Erivanski' Grenadier Regiment, the oldest unit in the Russian army. The Tsar and his entourage are watching manœuvres at Krasnoe Selo, August 1913.

129 *below*　The Grand Duchesses watching the manœuvres from the 'Tsar's Mound'. They are observing (**128** *left*) a Regiment of Cossack Guards spurring forward in a massed charge.

130 *overleaf*　The Emperor samples the soldiers' food during a visit to the Sapper Guards Regiment at Krasnoe Selo, August 1913.

In an environment as military-minded as that in which the children of Nicholas II grew up, it was natural that even the daughters should be interested in military affairs. When they reached a suitable age, each was 'given' her own regiment—Olga was Chief of the 3rd 'Elisavetgradski' Hussars and Tatiana of the 8th 'Vosnesenski' Lancers. Mounted and in their respective uniforms, they reviewed 'their' regiments at a mounted full-dress parade at Peterhof on 5 August 1913. Their grandmother, Marie Feodorovna, noted: 'How delighted Olga, and Tatiana must be to be able to review their regiments on horseback. I regret not to be able to be there and watch them do it.' After the parade, the Emperor and his two daughters invited the officers of the regiments to lunch in the Grand Palace at Peterhof.

131 The rehearsal a few days before the parade.

132-3 The rehearsal for the parade. Alexei (**133**) looks on in envy of his sisters, with members of the Imperial family.

The Lancers outside the Palace after lunch.

135 *left* Tatiana and Olga in regimental uniform.

136 *below* The Hussars outside the Palace after lunch.

The Emperors of Russia visited Poland every autumn for two to four weeks, to shoot and hunt. There were three hunting-lodges: Bielovezh and Spala were each visited in turn for one or two weeks and Skernevitsi usually only for a day or two. Large numbers of soldiers were brought in to act as beaters during the shoots, less often during the hunts. Sometimes an entire division would be pressed into service. Those so employed considered it a great honour and, consequently, every unit stationed in Poland was given an opportunity over the years to participate.

137 *left* The Emperor and his cousin, Grand Duke Nicholas Nikolaevich, inspect a fine kill—a European bison or aurochs—at Bielovezh. Only two herds of aurochs remained in existence at the beginning of this century, at Bielovezh and in the Caucasus. Both herds were then being well maintained and were rapidly expanding, but the First World War and the Russian Civil War made them virtually extinct in the wild.

138 *opposite* The Emperor at a shoot in Poland.

139 *below*   The Emperor inspects a Guard of Honour drawn from the 1st 'Volga' Terek Cossack Regiment before its departure for the Japanese War, Kremenchug, 5 May 1904. The figure with the bushy white moustache is the Minister of the Court. General V. A. Sukhomlinov, who rose to prominence after 1909, when he was made Minister of War, is following Nicholas II, his hand raised in salute.

140 *right*   The review of the 1st Brigade, 37th Infantry Division at Peterhof, 16 July 1904, before its departure to the Far East. The Emperor has just given the officers of the 148th 'Tsaritsyn' Infantry Regiment his blessing. His mother, the Dowager Empress Marie Feodorovna, stands beside her carriage, holding a dark parasol, and Empress Alexandra and her daughter Olga can be seen sitting in another carriage. This photograph was taken exactly two weeks before the birth of the Tsarevich Alexei.

4=Октября 1904г. Царское Село.

141 *above*   The fête of the Cossack Escort at Tsarskoe Selo,
4 October 1904. The Cossack Escort was part of the Imperial
Guard, but under the authority of the Commandant of the
Palace. This regiment provided the closest guard for the
Emperor and his family. At night they paced quietly outside
their bedroom doors and below their windows. The
inscription reads '4 October 1904. Tsarskoe Selo' and is in the
handwriting of the Emperor. It was taken from the Alexander
Palace in Tsarskoe Selo, when it was looted by the Germans
during the Second World War. It was then that the corner
of the picture was burnt. The last survivor of the group,
Prince A. V. Amilakhvari, seated third from right in front,
died in 1968.

142 *right*   Nicholas II about 1904.

On 30 July 1904 the long-awaited son and heir was born. He was named Alexis (Alexei) after Tsar Alexis Mikhailovich, son of the first Romanov Tsar and, of his predecessors, the one most admired by Nicholas II. As Russia was at war with Japan, all her soldiers were honorary godfathers to the child. It was almost without precedent in the history of Russia that an heir to the Throne should be born to a reigning Emperor, and the nation celebrated.

The discovery that the child suffered from haemophilia was a terrible blow to the Empress, for she realized that she was the transmitter of the disease. Until the abdication in 1917, she thought of little except to ease the child's suffering or find a cure. As a result, her own health suffered and she aged prematurely.

143 A postcard photograph of the Tsarevich Alexei which was distributed to the troops.

144 'Nicky & Alexei'.

145 'Alexandra & Alexei'.

A clash between Russia and Japan was almost inevitable by the turn of the century. Russia had expanded in the East, and the growth of her settlement and her territorial ambitions, as her southward path to the Balkans was frustrated, conflicted with Japan's own territorial ambitions on the Chinese and Asian mainland. War began in 1904 with a surprise torpedo attack on the Russian fleet in Port Arthur, which incapacitated the Russian navy in the East. An epic voyage was begun by the Russian Baltic fleet to traverse the world and equalize the balance of power in the East. The effort was in vain, as the fleet, after many misadventures *en route*, was annihilated by the Japanese in the Battle of the Tsushima Strait. On land the Russians fared no better and the army was crippled both by mismanagement and by the problem of conducting a war with only the Trans-Siberian Railway as a carrier of supplies from the West. The war ended in total defeat for Russia with the fall of Port Arthur in 1905, and the settlement of both countries' quarrels by the Treaty of Portsmouth.

As a result of the disastrous war, Russia's self-esteem received a severe blow and the Imperial Government collapsed, with the ensuing revolutionary outbreaks of 1905–6. Many demonstrators were shot in front of the Winter Palace in St Petersburg; the Emperor's uncle, Grand Duke Serge, was blown up by a revolutionary's bomb. The Black Sea fleet mutinied, and a railway strike developed into a general strike which paralysed the country. Nicholas, who was taken by surprise by the events, mixed his anger with bewilderment. He wrote to his mother after months of disorder:

> It makes me sick to read the news! Nothing but new strikes in schools and factories, murdered policemen, Cossacks and soldiers, riots, disorder, mutinies. But the ministers, instead of acting with quick decision, only assemble in council like a lot of frightened hens and cackle about providing united ministerial action . . . ominous quiet days began, quiet indeed because there was complete order in the streets; but at the same time everybody knew that something was going to happen—the troops were waiting for the signal, but the other side would not begin. One had the same feeling as before a thunderstorm in summer! Everybody was on edge and extremely nervous, and, of course, that sort of strain could not go on for long . . . We are in the midst of a revolution with an administrative apparatus entirely disorganised, and in this lies the main danger.

The chaotic situation in 1905 and 1906 limited Nicholas's travelling within Russia and abroad. Security requirements made it necessary for the Imperial family to stay, under guard, in their residences. The only escape open to them was to cruise on the *Standart* or *Polar Star* in the Gulf of Finland and to be satisfied with minor expeditions ashore on the almost completely deserted islands.

146 *above* After a shoot on one of the Finnish islands, 1905. Seated at the extreme right, next to the Empress, is Anna Vyrubova.

147 *left* The review at Peterhof, 30 August 1906. During the summer of 1906 armed revolutionaries arrived in Peterhof with the intention of assassinating the Tsar and any other suitable targets. He wrote to his mother: 'After you left, we had to sit here at Alexandria [Peterhof]—virtual prisoners. How shameful it is, even to speak about it! . . . those anarchist scoundrels, encouraged by their success, came here to Peterhof to hunt for me . . . the ringleaders were arrested yesterday, which was fortunate in view of today's inspection. But you will understand my feelings, my dear Mama, when I tell you I have been unable to go out riding or even outside the gate, and this at one's home—at Peterhof—usually so peaceful!' However, the inspection was able to take place as evidenced by this photograph; the Emperor wears the uniform of the Pavlovsky Guards.

148 Empress Alexandra and her sister
Princess Victoria of Battenberg at Peterhof,
August 1906.

149 The Empress and her two-year-old son
at Peterhof, August 1906.

150 *right* The fête of the Horse Guards Regiment at Tsarkoe Selo, 25 March 1907. The Emperor speaks to to his sister Olga as the Empress and their children look on. The Minister of the Court, Baron Freedericksz, was a former commander of the Horse Guards and he brought many of its officers into the Court Ministry and the Emperor's household.

151 *below* The festival of Her Majesty's Lancer Guards Regiment, Peterhof, 16 May 1907. The officer standing on the Empress's left is the regimental commander, Major-General A. A. Orlov, an old friend and comrade of the Emperor from the Hussars; he was soon to die in Egypt of tuberculosis.

152 While cruising in the Gulf of Finland at the end of August 1907, the *Standart* struck an uncharted rock and for a time seemed in danger of sinking. The Imperial family was quickly transferred to an accompanying vessel, the *Polar Star,* after which the cruise continued. Left to right: Marie, Anastasia, Alexei, Olga and Tatiana.

153 On one of the Finnish islands, September 1907. On the Emperor's right is Admiral Count Tolstoy, with Grand Duchess Anastasia sitting on his knee. The Tsarevich Alexei sits between his father and mother.

154 *above* Nicholas (in British naval uniform) with his
guest King Edward VII (in Russian naval uniform) aboard
the *Standart*, during the visit to Cowes, 1909. King Edward
made only one State visit to Russia. Left to right: Duke of
York (later George V), Princess Victoria, Empress Alexandra,
the Duke of Connaught, King Edward VII and Nicholas.

155 *right* Captain Chagin salutes as the Emperor samples the
sailors' food aboard the *Standart*, 1908.

156 *above left*   Alexei and his cousin Prince Louis of Battenberg (later Lord Mountbatten) in front of the 'datcha' at Alexandria-Peterhof.

157 *above right*   The Emperor, Princess Victoria of Battenberg, Grand Duchess Serge and Princess Louise of Battenberg on a visit to the pavilion on Olga Island in the lake of the park at New Peterhof.

158 *above left* Olga: 'She possessed a remarkably quick brain. She had good reasoning powers as well as initiative, a very independent manner, and a gift for swift and entertaining repartee': Pierre Gilliard, the Swiss tutor to the Imperial children. Source: *Thirteen Years at the Russian Court*, London, 1921.

159 *above centre* Tatiana 'was rather reserved, essentially well balanced, and had a will of her own, though she was less frank and spontaneous than her elder sister. She was not so gifted, either, but this inferiority was compensated by more perseverance and balance. She was very pretty, though she had not quite Olga Nicolaevna's charm': Pierre Gilliard.

160 *above right* Marie: 'a fine girl, tall for her age, and a picture of glowing health and colour. She had large and beautiful grey eyes. Her tastes were simple, and with her warm heart she was kindness itself. Her sisters took advantage somewhat of her good nature, and called her "fat little bow-wow". She certainly had the benevolent and somewhat *gauche* devotion of a dog': Pierre Gilliard.

161 *below left* Anastasia: 'very roguish and almost a wag. She had a very strong sense of humour and the darts of her wit often found sensitive spots. She was rather an *enfant terrible*, although this fault tended to correct itself with age. She was also extremely idle, though with the idleness of a gifted child': Pierre Gilliard.

162 *below right* The young Grand Duchesses: Marie, Olga, Anastasia and Tatiana, Peterhof, 1908.

During 1909 Nicholas II travelled widely. A State visit to Sweden was followed by less formal visits to France and England and another State visit to Italy. On the way to France and England, the *Standart* passed through the Kiel Canal. German Uhlans escorted them along the banks and Guards of Honour stood to attention at every landing. The Kaiser and his brother Prince Henry of Prussia came on board at Kiel to pay their respects, and the Grand Duke and Duchess of Hesse, Princess Henry and her two sons and two of the Battenberg children stayed on board for the trip through the Canal.

163 *above* The Empress and her daughters follow events on the bank as they pass through the Kiel Canal.

164 *right* The Tsarevich tastes the sailors' food as the Emperor, Admiral Nilov (back to camera) and Derevenko look on.

165-6 At the beginning of his two-day visit to France. Nicholas reviews the French fleet with President Fallières at Cherbourg, 18–19 July 1909.

168 The President and the Empress chat during a break.

169 *left* Nicholas and the French Admiral.

170 Father and son about 1910. The photograph appears to have been taken in the park at Tsarskoe Selo. The Emperor is wearing the uniform of the 4th 'Imperial Family' Rifle Guards and the Tsarevich that of an infantry soldier.

171 *above* The Emperor, Empress and
Tsarevich leave the Catherine Palace at
Tsarskoe Selo after a review of Boy
Scouts, 22 May 1910.

172 *right* Nicholas, 1910.

173-4 *above* The Emperor with his children on the *Standart*, 1910.

175 *left* Nicholas, Marie and Olga on a visit to Schloss Romrod, 1910.

176 A ceremony in the courtyard of the Catherine Palace at Tsarskoe Selo, March 1912. A loud noise during the playing of the National Anthem startled the commander of the Guard of Honour and he glanced away at the moment the photograph was taken. No one noticed the incident at the time but in due course a copy of the photograph found its way to his regimental commander and he was immediately placed under arrest.

Livadia, 1912

177 *above* The Emperor, Grand Duke Ernst Ludwig of Hesse and Captain Neverovski of the *Standart* watch a passing bird.

178 *centre left* The Empress and Princess Orbeliani as spectators on the tennis court.

179 *centre right* The Emperor and Lieutenant A. I. Butakov as tennis partners. Butakov was a well-liked officer of the *Standart* and the Emperor's usual and favourite tennis partner. He went to the front in 1914 with a battalion of the Garde Équipage and was killed soon after.

180 *left* The Emperor, Empress and young Prince Louis of Hesse on the beach near Livadia.

On the 'Day of White Flowers', set aside to raise money to support sanatoria in the Crimea.

181 *above* The Emperor of Russia sells towels embroidered by his wife and daughters and other handicrafts at a stand on the mole at Yalta, 20 April 1912. The *Standart* appears in the background.

182 *right* The Empress and Alexei collect funds. Olga and Tatiana stand behind her carriage with garlands of flowers; a white flower was given to those who made a contribution. The sailor is Alexei's guardian, Derevenko.

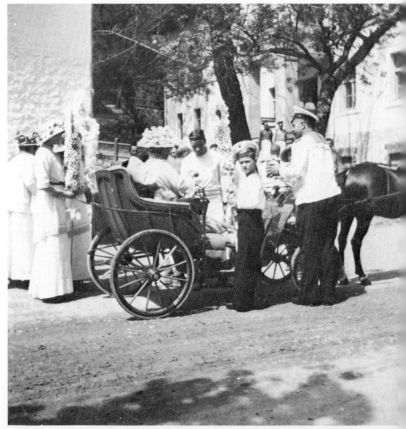

Pitkopas, Finland, August 1912

183 *above left*   Alexei with his nurse Tegleva.

184 *above right*   Alexei with the sailor Nagorny, who was responsible for looking after him.

185 *left*   Alexei with the ship's boys from the *Standart*.

In August 1912 the Emperor came to Moscow with his family to celebrate the centenary of Napoleon's defeat in Russia. The great symbolic act of the centenary was the 'Te Deum' and review on the field of Borodino, where the battle took place. Nicholas described the scene to his mother:

> Certainly the most remarkable days were the 25 and 26 of August at Borodino. A common feeling of deep reverence for our forebears seized *us* all there. No description of the battle can ever produce an impression comparable at all to the one which moves one on setting foot on the soil where the blood was shed of fifty-eight thousand of our brave men, killed or wounded in those two days of the battle of Borodino . . . a number of old men who still remember the coming of the French had been assembled and most important amongst them was the veteran Sergeant-Major Voitiniuk, one hundred and twenty-two years of age, who himself had fought in the battle! Just imagine, to be able to speak to a man who remembers everything, describes details of the action, indicates the place where he was wounded etc., etc.! I told them to stand next to us by the tent during the service and was able to watch them all through it. They knelt and got up quite easily some even without the help of their sticks!

186 The State visit to Moscow. The Emperor and Empress and the Tsarevich descend the Red Staircase, followed in procession by the other members of the Imperial family. A large cheering throng was crowded into the confined space of the Kremlin.

187 *opposite* The review of the Moscow Garrison on the Khodinski Field, 28 August 1912. The Emperor's page Semchevski follows his master into the pavilion during the ceremonies.

188 Alexei and his sisters watch from their carriage as the Emperor inspects a gathering of Moscow school-children in the Kremlin, August 1912.

189 At the centenary celebrations on the field of Borodino, 26 August 1912, the Emperor takes the salute at the march past led by the Palace Grenadier Company which wears the bearskins of Napoleon's Old Guard. The monument commemorates the battle.

Early in the autumn of 1912 the Emperor and his family went to Poland as usual. At Bielovezh the Tsarevich hurt himself while jumping out of a boat and at first the injury did not appear too serious. Soon he recovered enough for the family to move on as planned to the hunting-lodge at Spala. Shortly after they arrived there, Alexei again injured himself, and the pain was so severe that the child frequently expressed a wish to die. The doctors considered the possibility so likely that on one occasion they advised that death would occur within twenty-four hours. All preparations were made, a tent was erected on the lawn to serve as a temporary chapel, prayers were said day and night for the child's recovery and the doctors prepared the necessary bulletins.

Yet he did not die. The Empress was convinced that it was due to the intervention of a disreputable Siberian peasant, Grigory Efimovich Rasputin, a 'Man of God', whom she had known for six years.

The events at Spala are remarkable not only for Rasputin's increased influence following the recovery of the Tsarevich, but also for the manner in which the Imperial couple reacted. Few intimates and no stranger would have realized that anything extraordinary had occurred. Until the last few days before the final crisis, no public notice was taken of the illness. The

Emperor went out shooting and for walks in the forest. The Empress followed her usual routine. Life went on as normal.

There has been a great deal of speculation over the years as to why the family reacted as they did and why no public announcement was made of the cause of the child's illness. There were two basic reasons why nothing was said and why no one apart from a few intimates and the doctors knew anything about the illness. The first was that both parents believed that the illness was not a public matter. The second reason is more complicated. They were both deeply ashamed of the fact that the longed-for son and heir which the nation demanded of them was suffering from an illness with no known cure. To Nicholas, to whom the words of his oath meant more than anything, the knowledge that he had failed his country must have been intolerable. To Alexandra, the knowledge that she was the cause—inadvertently or not—of the physical suffering of the child and the emotional suffering of her husband must have been worse still.

190-1 The Emperor receives bread and salt from a deputation of local village elders at Bielovezh, September 1912.

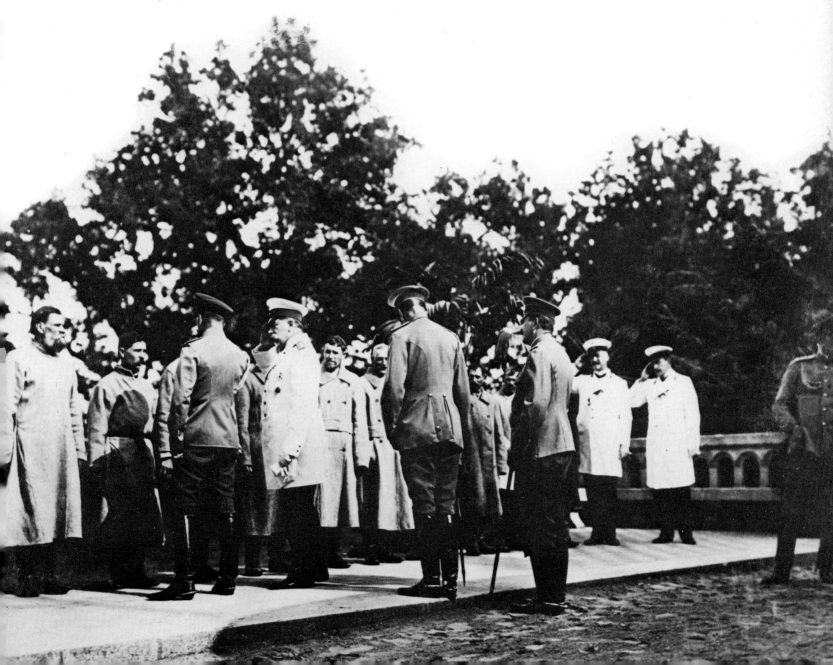

192 Leaving the church at Bielovezh after the service, September 1912. As the Tsarevich does not appear in the photograph, it must be assumed that it was taken after his fall.

193 During a walk in the forest with Major-General Prince Belosselsky, the Emperor replies to the greeting of soldiers of one of the units employed in providing security for the hunt at Bielovezh, September 1912.

194 *above left*   Lunch in the forest.

195 *below left*   The Emperor returns to
the hunting-lodge at Spala after the
hunt, October 1912.

196 *above*   Nicholas's trophy.

197 *above* The service of thanksgiving
to celebrate the recovery of the Tsarevich
at Spala, 23 October 1912. The
Emperor and Empress greet members of
the suite on their arrival.

198 *right* The Emperor poses with his
gentlemen on the steps of the hunting-
lodge after the service.

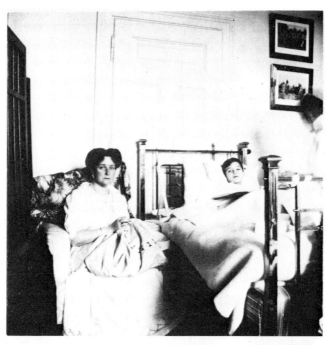

199 The Tsarevich in bed at the beginning of his recovery, Spala, late October 1912. The Empress, exhausted, sits beside him.

200 His health much improved, Alexei is taken for a ride accompanied by Gilliard, Petrov, Derevenko, a servant, and two court policemen. Spala, November 1912.

201-4 Towards the end of the stay in Poland, the Emperor attended another shoot, accompanied by Grand Duchess Olga. A young officer of the St Petersburg Guards Regiment, whose regiment was part of the guard for the shoot, took this series of photographs.

205-13 The Empress and her children at Alexandria-Peterhof, 1913. The photographs were taken in a room at the top of the tower of their house, looking out over the Gulf of Finland.

214 *above* Alexei and Tatiana on the way to a review of recruits, escorted by Her Majesty's Lancer Guards at Tsarskoe Selo, 1913.

Livadia, 1913 *opposite*

215 *above left* The Empress and her son.

216 *above right* Alexei having a mud bath. Dr Derevenko describes the treatment to the Empress as the sailor Derevenko and Dr Botkin look on.

217-19 *centre left and right and below left* Nicholas and his family, together with his personal suite.

220 *below right* Tea with the Empress. Left to right: Marie, the Empress, Olga, Engineer Lieutenant I. M. Mochalov, Commander N. P. Sablin, Tatiana and Anastasia.

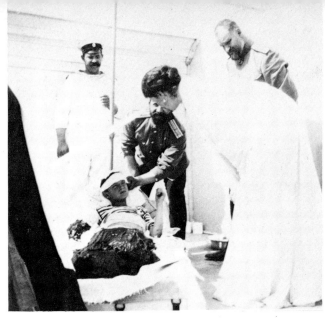

221 *left*   Alexei receives a deputation
from the Ataman Cossack Guards
Regiment, of which he was Chief.
The officers (left to right) are the Emperor's
aide-de-camp Captain Mikheev,
General Count Ignat'ev (attached
to the person of the Tsarevich), and Senior
Colonel D. P. Sazonov.

222 *right*   The Emperor and Count
Freedericksz, Livadia, 1913.

On the tennis court at Livadia

223 *above left*   Grand Duchess Anastasia.

224 *above right*   Grand Duchess Tatiana on the umpire's seat.

225 *left*   The Emperor (third from left) seated with his tennis companions: Lieutenant N. N. Rodionov, Lieutenant A. I. Butakov and Commander N. P. Sablin.

226–32 The excursion to the 'Red Rock' in the Crimea, 8 May 1914. Accompanied only by the tutor Gilliard, Lieutenant Baron G. N. Taube of the *Standart*, the sailor Derevenko and a Cossack orderly, the Emperor took his son for a much needed outing away from the restrictions and confinement of the Palace and the Court. 'There was still plenty of snow about and Alexei had huge fun sliding on it. He ran round us, skipping about, rolling in the snow and picking himself up, only to fall again a few seconds later . . . The Tsar watched his son's frolics with obvious pleasure. You could see how happy he was to realize that the boy had recovered the health and strength of which he had been deprived so long. Yet he was still haunted by the fear of accidents and every now and then he intervened to moderate his transports. Although he never so much as referred to the disease to which the heir was a victim, it caused him perpetual anxiety and concern.' Pierre Gilliard: *Thirteen Years at the Russian Court.*

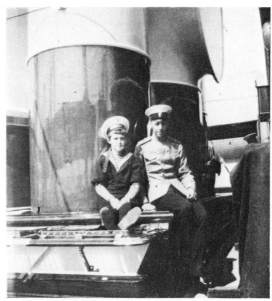

233 *above left* Aboard the *Standart*, June 1914; Anastasia and Lieutenant N. N. Rodionov.

234 *above right* Alexei and Baron G. N. Taube.

235 *centre left* Marie and Colonel Drenteln.

236 *centre right* Grand Duchess Marie.

237 *left* Tatiana and Alexei.

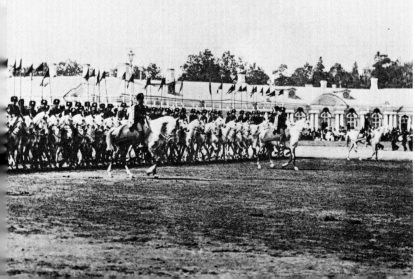

238 *above* A parade in honour of the King of Saxony at Tsarskoe Selo, June 1914. The King was much embarrassed when two months later he was forced by the Kaiser to declare war on his recent host.

239 *left* The march past of His Majesty's Hussar Guards before the Emperor and the King of Saxony.

The State visit of President Raymond Poincaré of France to St Petersburg at the beginning of July 1914 was the last, but perhaps the most important, of the series of visits begun in the 1890s. The President arrived off Kronstadt on 7 July on the *France* and immediately transferred on a Russian cutter to the old paddle-wheel Imperial yacht *Alexandria*, on which the Emperor was waiting.

After spending the 8th in St Petersburg, paying official visits and receiving deputations of Frenchmen living in Russia, on the 9th he attended a great luncheon given by the Emperor at Peterhof for the officers of the French squadron; the President then went by train with the Emperor to Krasnoe Selo to inspect the camp and attend the evening service and retreat.

The 10th was the final day of the visit, marked by the grand review of the Imperial Guard with some 100,000 men marching past to French military marches. In the evening the President gave a farewell dinner to his hosts on the *France*. A communiqué was agreed upon which stated the common attitude of the two states to current problems. The President bid his hosts farewell and sailed away.

The next morning, news of the Austrian ultimatum to Serbia was received.

240-1 The arrival of the Emperor and President Poincaré
on the *Alexandria* at Peterhof, 7 July 1914.

242 *below*   The Emperor (on horseback) and the President on their arrival at Krasnoe Selo, 9 July 1914. In the carriage with the President are the Empress and the two youngest Grand Duchesses; the carriage made a circuit of the camp, passing through lines of cheering soldiers.

243 *below right*   At the beginning of the evening ceremony, the regimental adjutants and regimental sergeant-majors report to the Emperor.

244 *right* Having taken the salute of the officers of the Imperial Guard after the grand review on 10 July, the Emperor rides back to join the President.

245 The Emperor escorts the President from the pavilion on the 'Tsar's Mound' from which Poincaré had been watching the review.

If anyone had inquired in 1914 what Russia most needed, the obvious answer would have been 'Peace!' Her internal situation had altered greatly in the previous ten years: a disastrous war foolishly entered into, succeeded by equally disastrous revolutionary convulsions, was followed by seven years of recovery and expansion on an unprecedented scale. The land reforms of Prime Minister Stolypin, which aimed to end the social turmoil of the previous century, were taking effect at the time of his assassination in 1911, and a period of peace and stability would allow projects in every field of endeavour to be planned and consolidated. A time of tremendous expansion lay ahead.

It seems unlikely that any national leader was more aware of the dangers of war than Nicholas II. He did not envisage the Revolution and the collapse of the Empire, but he saw that Russia could only lose by involvement in a war which she was bound to enter by her alliance with France. Antipathy towards Austria-Hungary permitted no compromise with that State. Nicholas could only hold Russia back as long as possible while trying to dissuade the Kaiser from his rush to Armageddon. In 1914 the Tsar and the Kaiser were equally captives of their General Staffs and Foreign Ministries.

When Nicholas finally had to agree to mobilization, it was with the greatest misgivings. With sadness, not elation, he observed the enthusiasm of the crowds that greeted him in Petersburg and Moscow in those first days, even if the unity of the Empire—and it was at last truly united—was something to be thankful for.

246 The Emperor on the balcony of the Winter Palace at St Petersburg after the 'Te Deum', 20 July 1914. Pierre Gilliard noted in his diary: 'The Tsar . . . was a changed man. Yesterday's ceremony resolved into an impressive manifestation. When he appeared on the balcony of the Winter Palace the enormous crowd which had collected on the square fell on their knees and sang the Russian National Anthem. The enthusiasm of his people has shown the Tsar that this is unquestionably a national war.'

247　The Empress bids farewell to each of 'her' Lancers at Peterhof before their departure for the front, 21 July 1914.

248 The procession from the Grand Palace of the Kremlin to the Uspensky Cathedral for the 'Te Deum', Moscow, 5 August 1914. Gilliard noted in his diary: 'At eleven o'clock, when the Tsar appeared at the top of the Red Staircase, the huge crowd in the square gave him a magnificent reception. He came down slowly, with the Tsarina on his arm, and at the head of a long procession, crossed the bridge connecting the Palace with the Cathedral . . . and entered the Church amid a frantic outburst of cheering from the crowd.'

249 *left* The visit to the Troitsko-Sergievskaia monastery near Moscow, 8 August 1914.

250 *below* The Emperor inspects the graduation parade of the cadets of the Michael and Constantine Artillery Academies and the Nicholas Engineering Academy at Tsarskoe Selo, 24 August 1914. This ceremony, in the courtyard of the Catherine Palace, was one of the first of the accelerated wartime promotions of young officers badly needed to fill gaps in units at the front and those newly formed. Under normal circumstances, these young men would have remained in their academies until the following August. In peacetime the Emperor attended as many of these ceremonies as possible, but this would be one of the last—if not the last. There were too many other obligations to fulfil in wartime.

251 *below* The Emperor with the Commander-in-Chief, Grand Duke Nicholas Nikolaevich, and the Staff at Supreme Headquarters at Baranovichi, September 1914. Seated left to right: the Chaplain-in-Chief of the army and navy, Father Shavelski, General Ianushkevich, the Emperor, Grand Duke Nicholas Nikolaevich, General Ruszki, Quartermaster-General Danilov, Grand Duke Peter Nikolaevich. The officer with oriental features standing just to the right of Grand Duke Peter is Prince Tundutov, a direct descendant of Genghis Khan and hereditary ruler of the Kalmuks.

252 *left* The Emperor and his entourage at Baranovichi, September 1914. The Emperor described his visit to the Grand Duke Nicholas to his wife: 'How terrible it was parting from you and the dear children, though I know it was not for long. The first night I slept badly because the engines jerked the train roughly at each station. I arrived here the next day at 5.30; it was cold and raining hard. Nicolasha [Grand Duke Nicholas] met me at the station at Baranovichi, and then we were led to a charming wood in the neighbourhood, not far from his own train.' Left to right: Captain Sablin, the Emperor, Colonel Drenteln, General Voeikov and Colonel Naryshkin.

253 *below* Grand Duke Nicholas Nikolaevich and some of his officers at Baranovichi, September 1914. The Grand Duke stands talking to his Chief of Staff, General Ianushkevich. Grand Duke Peter stands on the left of the tree and Prince Peter of Oldenburg on the right of it. The Quartermaster-General, Danilov, stands with hands clasped behind his back at the right of the photograph.

254-5 The Emperor's arrival in Sevastopol on a military tour of inspection, January 1915. The Emperor liked to wear Cossack uniform, and being greeted by a Guard of Honour from a Kuban Cossack Infantry Regiment was a suitable occasion.

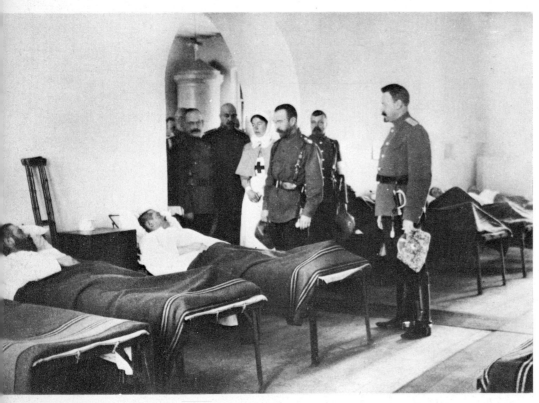

Христосованіе Государя Императора Николая II-го съ конвойцами
Ставка. Могилевъ 1915 года.

256 *above* A visit by the Emperor to his sister Olga's hospital at Rovno, 26 January 1915. Nicholas talks to a wounded soldier as General Voeikov and Colonel Drenteln stand in the doorway and Grand Duchess Olga looks on. The Grand Duchess was one of many members of the Imperial family who became nurses during the war.

257 *left* Nicholas greeting his Cossack Escort Easter, 1915

258 *right* Nicholas, early 1915.

259 The Emperor's visit to the fortress of Lemberg, 9 April 1915. He described Lemberg to Alix as 'a very handsome town, slightly resembling Warsaw, a great number of gardens and monuments, full of troops and Russians!'

260 The Emperor talks to the Governor of Occupied Galicia, General Count Bobrinski, at Lemberg, 9 April 1915.

261 *left* The Emperor and his cousin, Commander-in-Chief Nicholas Nikolaevich, who was replaced by the Emperor as Commander-in-Chief in 1915. Both he and the Emperor's mother were rescued from the Crimea after the Revolution by a British warship.

262 *above* Nicholas (far right) inspecting some of the damage to the former Austrian fortress at Przemysl. He described the fortifications of Przemysl as 'most interesting, colossal works— terribly fortified. Not an inch of ground remained undefended.'

263-7 A group of pictures taken on the Empress's balcony of the Alexander Palace at Tsarskoe Selo, 1915.

263 Nicholas.

264 Nicholas and Alexei.

265 Grand Duke Michael Alexandrovich.

266 Marie.

267 Anastasia.

268 *opposite left* Marie at Tsarskoe Selo, 1915.

269 *opposite right* Marie and Olga at Alexandria-Peterhof, 1915.

270 *left* Alexei and Joy at Tsarskoe Selo, 1915.

271 *above right* The funeral cortège of Grand Duke Constantine Constantinovich at Petrograd, June 1915. The Grand Duke, a famous poet and patron of the literary arts and owner of the magnificent Palace of Pavlovsk, was said to have died of a broken heart, having lost a son and son-in-law in the fighting. This was the last State funeral in Russia and the last one of a member of the Imperial family which the Emperor attended. Patriotism dictated that the name 'St Petersburg' should be changed to the Russian form of Petrograd.

272 *below right* The Emperor and his two eldest daughters join his mother and nephew Vasili for tea at the Elagin Palace, Petrograd, 1915.

273 *above left*   The Emperor and his son relax on the banks of the Dnieper and in the countryside near Mogilev, 1915.

274 *above right*   Gilliard, Alexei and Joy at the station in Pskov, 1 October 1915. It was on this spot that the Emperor abdicated exactly seventeen months later.

275 *centre*   The Emperor tries out a new tracked motor car in front of the Alexander Palace at Tsarskoe Selo as the Empress looks on. Grand Duchess Tatiana is seated in the back, the Emperor and Alexei (his face is hidden) on jump seats. The Master of the Horse, General von Grunwald, salutes.

276 *right*   The Emperor and the Chief of Staff, General Alekseev, at Mogilev.

277 *above left*   Alexei and Joy.

278 *above right*   Count Freedericksz, Grand Duke Dimitri Pavlovich and Alexei. Grand Duke Dimitri acted as the Emperor's serving aide-de-camp during much of 1915.

279 *left*   Alexei and his small cousins, Nikita, Rostislav, Dimitri and Vasili, the sons of Grand Duchess Xenia; they are out for a sleigh-ride in the park at Tsarskoe Selo, 1915.

Almost immediately after the outbreak of war, the Empress arranged for hospitals for the wounded to be opened in Tsarskoe Selo in buildings belonging to the Court.

The Empress, Olga and Tatiana took nursing courses and eventually became nursing sisters in what was called the Palace Hospital. This was for wounded officers and those sent there were usually guardsmen or of relatively good social background—a selection made by those at the front, not by the hospital. The staff of the hospital were not impressed by the humility and devotion of the Imperial nurses, and there were those who constantly criticized them behind their backs. Marie and Anastasia were considered too young to become nurses, but they were allowed to become patrons of another hospital for wounded lower ranks—also mainly from the Guard.

Above left to right and below right to left

280 Empress Alexandra as a nursing sister. This photograph was taken in 1915 and was a Christmas gift from the Empress to a wounded officer.

281 Olga as a nursing sister.

282 Tatiana and Olga at Tsarskoe Selo, 1915.

283-4 Two of a series of photographs numbered 1 to 9 and dated 1914 to 1916. The last two are undated. On the reverse of these the Empress had listed the name of each wounded officer; they were, it seems, a pocket record of her patients.

285 The Empress, Tatiana and Olga in their nurses' uniforms at Tsarskoe Selo, 1915.

286 Marie and Anastasia in the Palace Hospital.

287 Tatiana as a nursing sister.

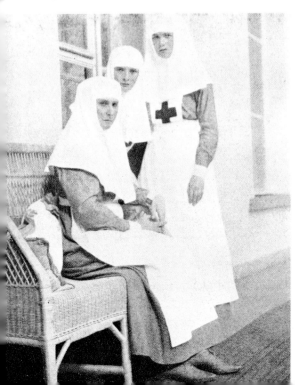

288-96 The construction of the snow tower in the park at Tsarskoe Selo, February 1916. Sailors from the Garde Équipage, which manned the Imperial yachts and also looked after the lakes in the Imperial parks, as well as representing the navy in the Imperial Guard, were called in to 'assist' the Emperor and his children in their effort to construct the tower. The main pleasure seems to have been derived from jumping off, which the Emperor (*below centre*) enjoyed as much as anyone else.

297 *above left*   Alexei, about to be taken for a sleigh-ride at Tsarskoe Selo in the winter of 1915–16. The child's wheel-chair is an obvious indication of the state of his health; he was subject to frequent recurrences of his illness through-out the war years.

298 *above right*   Alexei and Gilliard out for a ride.

299 *below left*   Joy, Gilliard and Alexei at Mogilev.

300 *below right*   Alexei and Joy at Mogilev.

Visit to the Black Sea Fleet at Sevastopol, 12 May 1916

301 *above*   The Emperor samples the sailors' food on the battleship *Empress Marie*.

302 *above right*   Alexei poses with an old friend from the *Standart*.

303 *above*   A visit to the synagogue of the Karaim Jews at Eupatoria.

304 *right*   Nicholas relaxing at Eupatoria in the Crimea, 16 May 1916.

On the Imperial train, 1916
305 *above left* Olga relaxes near the railway station at Mogilev.

306 *above right* Left to right: Grand Duke Dimitri Pavlovich, the Emperor, the Empress, Grand Duke Michael, Tatiana and Olga. In front sit Anastasia and Marie.

307 *above* In the dining car. Left to right: Alexei, General Voeikov, Professor Fedorov, Gilliard and Grabbe.

308 *right* The Emperor in his study on the train.

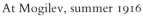

At Mogilev, summer 1916

Above, left to right

309 Nicholas inspects the squadron of the Cossack Escort after its return from front-line service.

310 Alexei and Gilliard.

311 Alexei in the garden of the Governor's house.

312 Nicholas relaxing in a pavilion.

Below, left to right

313 Gilliard and Alexei in the bedroom shared by the Emperor and his son in the Governor's residence.

314 At lunch. Left to right: Prince Eristov, aide-de-camp to Grand Duke George Mikhailovich, Prince Igor Constantinovich, the Emperor, Grand Duke George Mikhailovich, Alexei, General Voeikov, Count Grabbe, Prince Dolgoruki, Dr Derevenko, Gilliard.

315 Alexei with the Chiefs of the Allied Military Missions.

316 Alexei and the Belgian General Baron de Ryckl. They have swapped hats.

317 The Emperor and Alexei watch a tyre being changed on a car which has broken down near Mogilev, summer 1916.

318   Relaxing on the banks of the Dnieper near Mogilev, 1916. Left to right: Virubova, Mordvinov, Alexei, Sablin, the Empress and Olga.

319-23   The Emperor and his family on the Dnieper.

324–6 Nicholas and Alexei on the Dnieper.

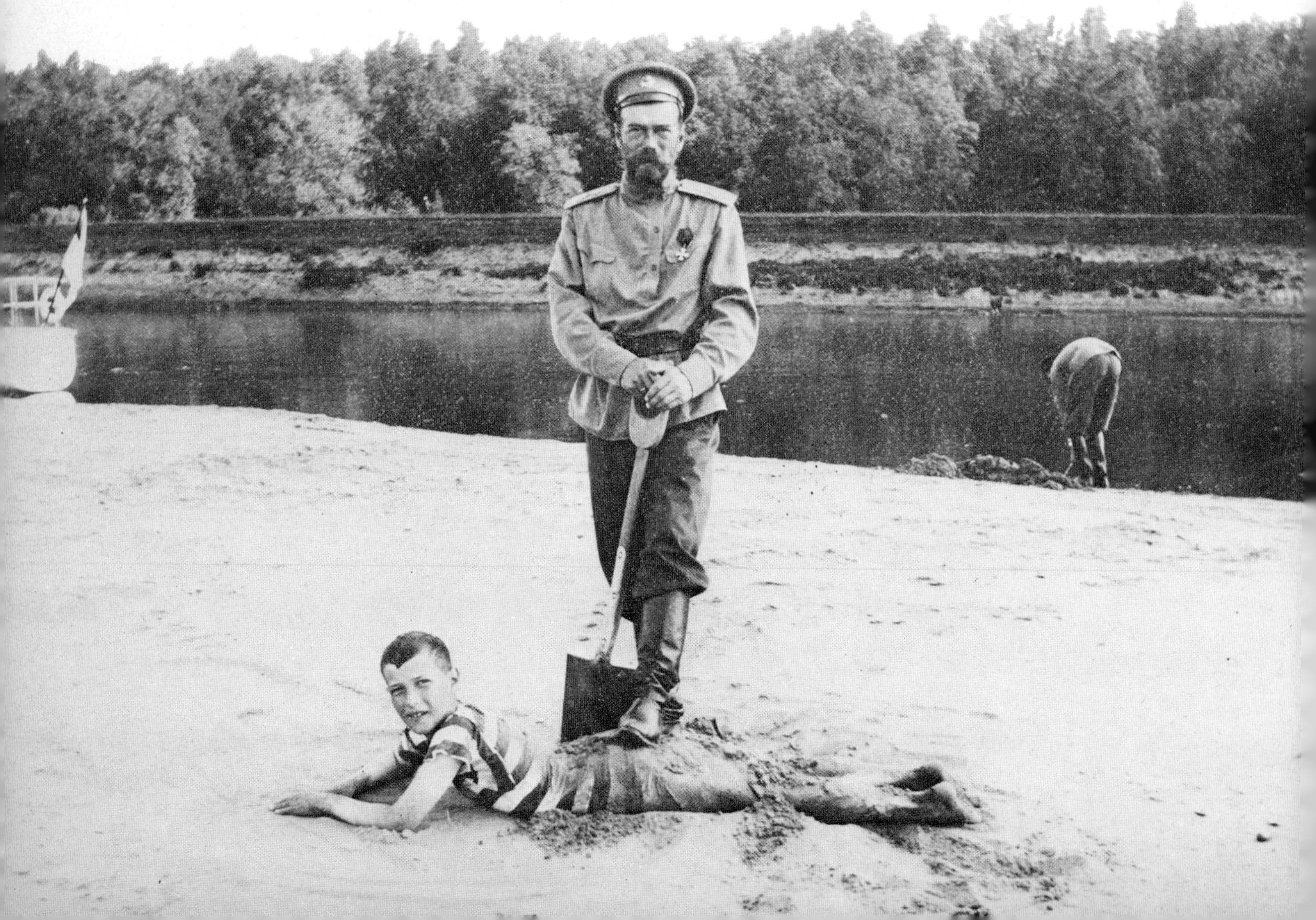

327 *below* Alexei in the water and Prince Igor
Constantinovich on the rope, watched by the Emperor, the
tutor Gilliard and Admiral Nilov.

328 *right* Nicholas and Alix.

329 *above left*   The Emperor and his children with officers of the Cossack Escort on the day of their regimental holiday at Mogilev, 4 September 1916.

330 *below left*   The Emperor and Tsarevich attend a review in the courtyard of the Catherine Palace at Tsarskoe Selo, 1916.

331 *above*   The feast day of the Order of St George. The Emperor, Empress and Alexei attend a gathering of the Knights of the Order in the People's Palace at Petrograd, 26 November 1916. In October 1915 the St George Council of the South-West Front voted to award the Emperor the Order of St George and his son a St George Medal as the result of their having 'come under enemy fire' earlier in the year. Knowing the Emperor's modesty, his childhood friend Prince Anatole Bariatinski was charged with the task of pressing the decoration on the Emperor in the name of the Army. At first refusing, because 'I am unworthy', Nicholas was persuaded to accept. He pinned on the Cross and took it off only a few days before the family was murdered, hiding it with his epaulettes in the Ipatiev house where they were later found.

Because of certain delicate feelings or perhaps through preoccupation with more immediate problems, no one appears to have taken any photographs of Nicholas II during the abdication crisis of February 1917 and the following week he spent in Mogilev, bidding the army farewell.

On 8 March 1917, the day of his last departure from Mogilev for Tsarskoe Selo, he went to say goodbye to his mother in her train—which was on the other side of the platform from his. While he was closeted alone with her, Empress Marie Feodorovna's lady-in-waiting remained outside on the platform. She took photographs of the former Empress's carriage, the Cossack Escort on guard at the door and the deserted snow-swept platform. They are the only photographic record remaining to us of that day and that week, but in his journal he wrote, with a mixture of anger and despair: 'On every side, treason, cowardice and skulduggery.'

He joined his family at Tsarskoe Selo: they were to remain united until the end.

332 The train of the Dowager Empress Marie Feodorovna at Mogilev, 8 March 1917.

Nicholas II abdicated—he believed—in the best interests of the Empire. He did so to prevent civil war, to keep the army out of politics and in a condition to help the Allies, and because he believed that the Provisional Government could rule Russia better than he had. He felt betrayed by his generals, particularly by his cousin, Grand Duke Nicholas Nikolaevich, who had turned their back on their Emperor. He criticized his brother Michael for not accepting the Throne. For five months he remained behind the fence of the Alexander Park, a prisoner in his own home, clearing the paths of snow and cutting wood.

333 Nicholas in March 1917.

334 The former Emperor and Captain Matve'ev of the 2nd 'Tsarskoe Selo' Rifle Guards Regiment Reserve Battalion clearing snow from the paths in the park at Tsarskoe Selo, March 1917. The Emperor became very fond of Matve'ev and presented him with his signed photograph on the morning of their departure for Siberia, saying that he hoped it would not cause difficulties for him in the future.

335 Breaking up the ice on the canal in the park at Tsarskoe Selo, April 1917.

At Tsarskoe Selo

Above, left to right

336 Nicholas cutting a wood with his servant, Zhuravski.

337 Tatiana with a young officer of the Guard, May 1917.

338 Alix and Tatiana.

Centre, left to right

339 A wood-cutting party, April 1917. Nicholas sits in front, Anastasia beside him. On either side of Anastasia, Prince Dolgoruki (wearing a cap) and Zhuravski. The others are an officer and soldier of the Guard and two Palace servants.
Gilliard noted in his diary: 'To occupy our leisure now that we have finished our work on the garden, we have asked and obtained permission to cut down the dead trees in the park, so we go from place to place, followed by a guard which moves when we move. We are beginning to be quite skilful wood-cutters.'

340 Alexei with an ensign of the Guard.

341 Nicholas and Dr Derevenko working in the garden, 17 May 1917.

342 Anastasia, Tatiana, Olga and Marie, May 1917. Gilliard noted in his diary: 'As the Grand Duchesses were losing all their hair as a result of their illness, their heads have been shaved. When they go out in the park they wear scarves arranged so as to conceal the fact. Just as I was going to take their photographs, at a sign from Olga they all suddenly removed their headdress. I protested but they insisted, much amused at the idea of seeing themselves photographed like this and looking forward to seeing the indignant surprise of their parents.'

Below, left and right

343-4 Nicholas and Anastasia, April 1917.

In July 1917, attempts to send the family to England having failed, the Provisional Government decided to get them away from the capital for their own safety, as there was concern that a revolutionary mob might try to seize them. They were kept sitting up all night to leave on the morning of 1 August for Tobolsk in Siberia. Like so many political prisoners in Russian history, Russia's last Emperor was now being sent to the other side of the Urals.

The journey was interesting and their new 'home' was at first not too unpleasant. As winter passed and the Bolshevik takeover succeeded finally in catching up with them, their circumstances rapidly deteriorated. In the end, their only fear was that for some reason Nicholas might be made to sign the Treaty of Brest-Litovsk. This he swore he would never do.

Nicholas and his family stayed nearly eight months in the comparative calm of Tobolsk. But as the balance of political power in Russia changed, and the Bolsheviks began to gain the upper hand, the family's position became more precarious. On 26 April 1918 Nicholas and Alix were transferred, in conditions of acute discomfort, to the town of Ekaterinburg in the Urals: the children followed a month later. Ekaterinburg was in the hands of the Bolsheviks, who commandeered the house of a merchant, Ipatiev, to be the last residence of Nicholas and his family. Early in the morning of 18 July the family was told to make themselves ready for a new journey to a more secure location: they were told to wait in a semi-basement room bare of any furniture. Three chairs were brought to make their waiting less uncomfortable. After a short wait, an execution squad entered the room and dispatched the family and the few attendants left with them in a fusillade of pistol shots.

345 The Governor's house at Tobolsk, August 1917.

346 *above*   Nicholas's study in the Governor's house.

347 *above right*   Alix's corner of the drawing room.

348 *right*   The drawing room.

At Tobolsk

Above, left to right

349   Nicholas and his children, September 1917: Tatiana, Olga, an unidentified child, Alexei, Nicholas and Anastasia.

350   Anastasia in her bedroom

351   Kolia Derevenko (the son of Dr Derevenko), Gilliard and Alexei on the steps of the Governor's house.

Below, left to right

352   Tatiana and an unidentified child.

353   Alexei on the balcony of the Governor's house, winter 1917–18.

354   One of the guards.

355   Nicholas and Gilliard sawing wood, March–April 1918.

215

Nicholas's character was a curious mixture of the complex and the simple; of all the analyses made of him, perhaps the most apt is that of Count Paul Benckendorff, who served at the Court of Nicholas, his father and grandfather. He wrote:

I was attached to the Emperor sincerely, and with all my heart. He was very young when he ascended the throne, with no experience of life or of affairs, and his character never had a chance of being formed. To the end of his life he lacked balance, nor could he grasp the principles that are necessary for the conduct of so great an empire. Hence his indecision, his limitations and the fluctuations which lasted throughout his reign. He was very intelligent, understood things at once, and was very quick, but he did not know how to reconcile his decisions with the fundamental political principles which he entirely lacked. Very kind-hearted, he was always ready to do a service, or to do anything that he was asked to do, sometimes without ascertaining whether it were feasible, and whether his decision might not be contrary to principles, whose violation would do more harm than good.

During the last years of his reign there was often talk of the influence, political and other, that Grigory Rasputin had exercised over their Majesties. Neither the Emperor nor the Empress ever mentioned him to me. I am convinced that the political influence of Rasputin was *nil*. The appointment of ministers, which, during the latter years, proved so fatal, can be explained otherwise, and if certain persons thought it necessary to approach that person for their private ends, they may have derived personal advantage, but he never had any influence on the course of political events.

He knew how to work on the religious sentiments of the Empress, who—as so often happens to persons of the Protestant religion who are converted to the Orthodox or the Catholic religion, and go to extremes—attached great importance to the outward forms of worship, and went so far as to take interest in local superstitions. The Emperor, I am certain, did not share these views, and if he gave the Empress a free hand in these matters, it was because he was jealous for the peace of his married life; besides which he had no time to arrange things in the way he would have wished.

In his private life he was touchingly kind to those near him. Easy of access, he never refused to listen to those who wished to see him, in spite of the number of papers he had to read every day. His family life was exemplary. He adored the Empress and his children: the heir-apparent—the little Grand Duke—was the especial object of his affection. His tardy birth, the poor state of his health, made him the idol of his parents. I often heard the Emperor say, in times of trouble during his reign, that he would accept all sufferings if he could leave Russia in order and prepare for his son an easy and a happy reign.

He had retained happy memories of the all too short periods in his youth when he had served in regiments, and the only treat he allowed himself was to take part from time to time in the dinners of the regiments of the Guard. He liked above all things to talk to the officers about the details of their service, and of their life in the garrisons.

He was temperate in his tastes: he ate little, drank but little wine, caring little for sport and riding. He felt a real craving for action, and was fond of walking and violent exercise; but his real affection was for his family, with which he was identified, and which was always the object of his unique adoration. Intelligent, good, well-meaning, his character did not allow him to respond to the gigantic events of the closing years of his reign. Weary and over-burdened as he was, these events crushed him.
(From *Last Days at Tsarskoe Selo*, London, 1927.)

356

Chronology

1868
6 May
Birth at Winter Palace, St Petersburg, of future Emperor Nicholas II, son of Tsarevich Alexander and Marie Feodorovna.

1869
26 May
Birth of Alexander Alexandrovich, younger brother of Nicholas, who died 20 April 1870.

1871
27 April
Birth of George Alexandrovich.

1872
25 May
Birth in Darmstadt of daughter to Princess Alice (daughter of Queen Victoria) and Grand Duke Louis IV of Hesse and the Rhine, christened Alix.

1873
June
Informal visit to England of Tsarevich Alexander and Marie Feodorovna with Nicholas and George and small entourage. Stay with Prince and Princess of Wales at Marlborough House.

1875
25 March
Birth of Xenia Alexandrovna.

1878
22 November
Birth of Michael Alexandrovich.

1881
1 March
Assassination of Emperor Alexander II in St Petersburg

1882
1 June
Birth of Olga, second daughter of Alexander III and Marie Feodorovna.

1883
27 May
Coronation of Emperor Alexander III and Empress Marie Feodorovna in Moscow.

1884
6 May
Ceremonies in Winter Palace, St Petersburg, celebrating coming of age of Tsarevich, culminating in his taking oath before assembled Court.
4 September
Emperors of Austria, Germany and Russia meet at Skernevitsi, an Imperial hunting-lodge.

1887
23 June
Nicholas begins military service as Second Lieutenant in 1st 'His Majesty's' Company of Preobrajensky Regiment, with whom he remained until 11 August 1887.

1888
17 June
Nicholas promoted commander of 1st 'His Majesty's' Company; continues in that position until 11 August.
7 July
Emperor Wilhelm II of Prussia visits Peterhof.
15 July
Great celebration, attended by Imperial family, in Palace Square, St Petersburg, on 900th anniversary of introduction of Christianity into Russia.
17 October
Train carrying Alexander III and family derailed in Kharkov province; it was completely wrecked and many killed. Only strength of Emperor, who supported collapsing carriage roof on his shoulders, prevented death of entire family.

1889
18 January
Grand Duke Louis IV of Hesse and the Rhine and youngest daughter Alix visit Grand Duke and Duchess Serge Alexandrovich in St Petersburg.
6 May
Emperor appoints Tsarevich a member of State Council and Committee of Ministers.
22 June
Nicholas begins service as subaltern in 1st 'His Majesty's' Squadron of His Majesty's Hussar Guards Regiment.
October
Nicholas attends wedding of his cousin Crown Prince Constantine of Greece.

1890
1 January
Nicholas promoted commander of 1st 'His Majesty's' Squadron; serves in that capacity from end June until completion of manœuvres at Krasnoe Selo in August, where Emperor Wilhelm II was a guest.
23 October
Nicholas and his brother George leave Gatchina for Vienna and Trieste to join *Pamiat Azova* for trip to the East. Main event of voyage was to have been laying of cornerstone of Trans-Siberian Railway near Vladivostok. Instead, it occurred in Otsu in Japan on 29 April 1891 when Nicholas was attacked by Japanese police officer.

1891
During summer camp of Imperial Guard, Nicholas commands 1st Section of 1st 'His Majesty's' Battery of Horse Guards Artillery, position he holds throughout 1892.

1893
1 January
Nicholas promoted commander of 1st Battalion of Preobrajensky Regiment with rank of Colonel.

July
Nicholas visits England for marriage of his cousin Duke of York (later King George V) to Princess Mary of Teck. During summer camp of Imperial Guard, Nicholas in active command of 1st Battalion.

1894
2 April
Nicholas leaves Gatchina with other members of Imperial family for wedding in Coburg (6 April) of Grand Duke Ernst Ludwig of Hesse and the Rhine to Princess Victoria of Saxe-Coburg-Gotha.
8 April
Nicholas engaged to Princess Alix of Hesse-Darmstadt at Coburg. After two weeks together, engaged couple part; Princess Alix goes to Windsor to stay with grandmother, Nicholas returns to Russia.
3 June
Accompanied only by Prince D. B. Golitsyn and a few servants, Nicholas sails on *Polar Star* for England (where he lands on 8th). Staying in turn with Prince and Princess Louis of Battenberg, Queen Victoria, and Prince and Princess of Wales, he spends most of his time with Princess Alix. On 12 July rejoins *Polar Star* to return to Russia.
25 July
Wedding at Peterhof of Grand Duchess Xenia to Grand Duke Alexander Mikhailovich.
8 August
Grand Review of regiments and brigades in camp at Krasnoe Selo by Emperor Alexander III; farewell to his Guards.
10 August
Launching of battleship *Admiral Seniavin* in presence of Emperor, Empress, Nicholas; Alexander III's last public engagement.
18 August
Departure of Emperor, Empress and children Nicholas, Michael and Olga for Bielovezh.
3 September
Imperial party leave Bielo for Spala.

8 September
Nicholas leaves Spala for Darmstadt, but recalled almost immediately after arrival.
17 September
Imperial party leave Spala for Crimea; bulletin issued stating that Emperor's health required warmer climate; that he was to go to Livadia.
21 September
Imperial party arrive in Livadia.
20 October
Emperor Alexander III dies.
27 October
Funeral cortège leaves Livadia with Black Sea Fleet acting as escort. New Emperor and family travel with body from Livadia to Sevastopol and from there by train to Moscow and St Petersburg.
1 November
Funeral train arrives in St Petersburg; Emperor's body carried in procession to Cathedral in the Fortress for lying-in-state.
7 November
Funeral of Emperor Alexander III.
14 November
Wedding in Winter Palace Church of Emperor Nicholas II and Grand Duchess Alexandra Feodorovna, now Empress.
17 November
Emperor resumes work, receiving Ministers in the morning and working with them exactly as his father had done.

1895
17 January
Gathering of leaders of the nobility, zemstvos and towns in the Nicholaevski Hall of Winter Palace, addressed by Emperor.
24 April
Review of Imperial Guard on Field of Mars in St Petersburg, Emperor's first since accession.
26–31 July
Emperor and Empress attend manœuvres at Krasnoe Selo.
31 August
Emperor and Empress move into Alexander Palace at Tsarskoe Selo.

3 November
Birth of Grand Duchess Olga at Tsarskoe Selo.

1896
6 May
Arrival of Emperor and Empress in Moscow for Coronation.
9 May
State entrance of Emperor into Moscow.
14 May
Coronation of Emperor Nicholas II.
18 May
Great review on Khodinski Field in Moscow.
August
State visits to Emperors of Austria and Germany in Vienna and Breslau.
September
Private visit to Denmark.
23–29 September
State visit to France.
4–15 October
Visit to Queen Victoria at Balmoral.

1897
15–18 April
State visit of Emperor Franz Joseph of Austria.
29 May
Birth of Grand Duchess Tatiana at Peterhof.
21–29 June
State visit of King of Siam.
26 July–1 August
State visit of Emperor and Empress of Germany.
11–14 August
State visit of President of France.
20–27 August
Visit to Warsaw and other areas of Poland, many reviews and parades.

1899
14 June
Birth of Grand Duchess Marie at Peterhof.
23 June
Grand Duke George Alexandrovich dies at Abas Tuman in Caucasus.

1900
1–23 April
Emperor and Empress visit Moscow.

1901
5 June
Birth of Grand Duchess Anastasia at Peterhof.
27 July
Wedding of Grand Duchess Olga Alexandrovna and Duke Peter Alexandrovich of Oldenburg at Gatchina.
21–28 August
Visit to Denmark.
28 August–2 September
While Empress goes to visit sister, Emperor joins Emperor Wilhelm II to observe German naval exercises.
5–9 September
Visit to France to attend manœuvres at Rheims and grand review at Chalons-sur-Marne.

1902
7–10 May
State visit of President of France.
30 June–4 July
State visit of King of Italy.
23 July
Emperor visits Reval for naval exercises.
24–26 July
Emperor of Germany visits Reval for Russian naval exercises.
29 August–5 September
Emperor attends grand manœuvres at Kursk. Shah of Persia guest of honour at parade of 94,000 men on 5 September.

1903
October
Informal visit to Emperor of Austria.

1904
Outbreak of Russo-Japanese War.

6 April
Survivors of *Variag* and *Koreits*, two warships sunk by the Japanese at beginning of war, return to St Petersburg and march through streets lined with cheering crowds to Winter Palace, where Emperor receives them.
8 June
Emperor attends funeral in St Petersburg of assassinated Governor-General of Finland, General N. I. Bobrikov.
18 July
Emperor attends funeral in St Petersburg of assassinated Minister of the Interior, V. K. von Pleve.
30 July
Birth of Tsarevich Alexei at Peterhof.
11 August
Tsarevich christened at Peterhof.
26–27 September
Emperor, Empress and Tsarevich inspect Baltic Fleet at Reval before departure for Far East.

1905
9 January
Troops who were ordered to halt them fire into processions of people carrying petitions to Emperor whom they believed to be in Winter Palace (he had been living in Tsarskoe Selo since end of previous September). Estimates of dead ranged from eighty-seven to 'many thousands' (former figure probably correct); day since known as 'Bloody Sunday'.

1906
16 January
King Christian IX of Denmark (Apapa) dies.
27 April
State Opening of Duma in Winter Palace.

1907
21–24 July
Visit to German Emperor at Swinemunde to observe German naval exercises.

1908
27 May
Visit off Reval, on board their yachts, of Russian Imperial and British Royal Families.
14–15 July
State visit off Reval, on board their yachts, of President of France to Emperor of Russia.

1909
27 June
200th Anniversary celebrations of Battle of Poltava attended by Emperor and all regiments that took part (on Russian side).
12 July
Imperial family depart on *Standart* from Peterhof for Hemmelmark (14–16 July) and private visit to Prince and Princess Henry of Prussia, Kiel Canal (16 July), Cherbourg (18–19 July) and visit to President of France, Cowes (20–22 July) and British Royal Family.
11–13 October
Emperor visits King and Queen of Italy at Racconigi.

1911
1 September
Prime Minister, P. A. Stolypin, shot during intermission of opera *Tsar Sultan*, attended by Emperor and two eldest daughters; dies on 5th.
15 October
Wedding in Vienna of Grand Duke Michael Alexandrovich and Natalia Sergeevna Vulfurt, formerly Mamontov, née Sheremetevski. (Emperor issues Imperial ukase giving her title of Countess Brassov.)

1912
21–23 June
German Emperor visits Emperor Nicholas at Baltic port in Gulf of Finland.

1913
21 February
Service in Kazan Cathedral in St Petersburg attended by entire Imperial family to commemorate tricentenary of Romanov rule.
7–12 May
Emperor visits Berlin for wedding of German Emperor's daughter Princess Victoria-Louise and Duke of Braun-schweig-Lunenburg.
15–28 May
Imperial family visit old Russian towns as part of tricentenary.

1914
9 February
Wedding in St Petersburg of Emperor's niece Princess Irene Alexandrovna and Prince Felix Youssoupov.
25 March
Imperial family depart for Crimea.
31 May–2 June
State visit to Romania.
5 June
Imperial family return to Tsarskoe Selo from Crimea and Romania.
6–9 June
State visit of King of Saxony.
7–10 July
State visit of President Poincaré of France.
20 September
Emperor leaves Tsarskoe Selo for first of many and lengthy visits to the Front.

1915
24 August
Emperor takes over as Commander-in-Chief of the armies.

1916
9 February
Emperor visits State Duma and State Council at beginning of their sessions.
16 December
Assassination of Rasputin.

1917
22 February
Emperor leaves Tsarskoe Selo for army headquarters at Mogilev.
23 February
Strikes begin in Petrograd.
28 February
Emperor leaves Mogilev to return to Tsarskoe Selo, believing he would be in a better position there to direct restoration of order in capital.
1 March
Unable to proceed direct to Tsarskoe Selo, Emperor's train redirected to Pskov.
2 March
Acting under great moral pressure, Nicholas II abdicates throne for himself and his son.
3 March
Nicholas leaves Pskov to return to Mogilev. Grand Duke Michael refuses to accept throne until called upon to do so by Constituent Assembly.
4 March
Dowager Empress arrives in Mogilev to see her son.
8 March
Arrest of former Empress by General Kornilov on orders of Provisional Government.
8 March
Nicholas signs farewell to army (which Provisional Government would not allow to be published) and boards train for Tsarskoe Selo. Placed under arrest by Commissioner of Provisional Government.
9 March
Former Emperor arrives in Tsarskoe Selo.
31 July
Imperial family leave for Tobolsk.
6 August
Imperial family arrive in Tobolsk.

1918
13 April (26 April n.s.)
The former Emperor and Empress and Grand Duchess Marie leave Tobolsk for unknown destination.

17 April (30 April n.s.)
Arrival in Ekaterinburg.
7 May (20 May n.s.)
Remaining children leave Tobolsk.
10 May (23 May n.s.)
Remaining children arrive at Ekaterinburg.
5 July (18 July n.s.)
Murder of Imperial family in early hours of morning. Later the same day Grand Duke Michael and his secretary Johnson murdered near Perm.

Genealogy

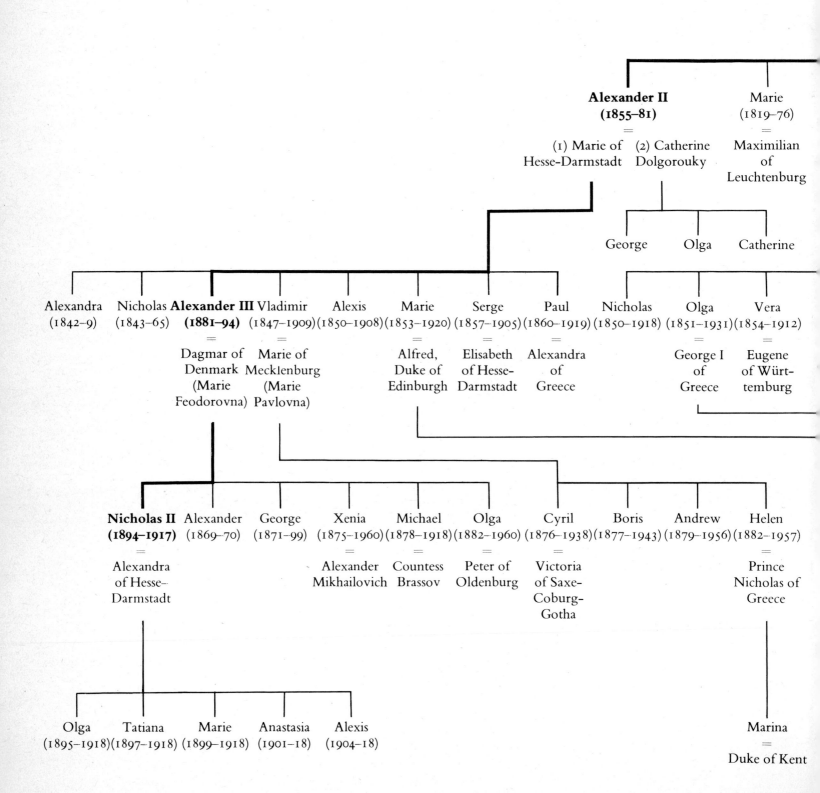

Alexander II (1855–81) = (1) Marie of Hesse-Darmstadt (2) Catherine Dolgorouky

Marie (1819–76) = Maximilian of Leuchtenburg

George　Olga　Catherine

Alexandra (1842–9)

Nicholas (1843–65)

Alexander III (1881–94) = Dagmar of Denmark (Marie Feodorovna)

Vladimir (1847–1909) = Marie of Mecklenburg (Marie Pavlovna)

Alexis (1850–1908)

Marie (1853–1920) = Alfred, Duke of Edinburgh

Serge (1857–1905) = Elisabeth of Hesse-Darmstadt

Paul (1860–1919) = Alexandra of Greece

Nicholas (1850–1918)

Olga (1851–1931) = George I of Greece

Vera (1854–1912) = Eugene of Württemburg

Nicholas II (1894–1917) = Alexandra of Hesse–Darmstadt

Alexander (1869–70)

George (1871–99)

Xenia (1875–1960) = Alexander Mikhailovich

Michael (1878–1918) = Countess Brassov

Olga (1882–1960) = Peter of Oldenburg

Cyril (1876–1938) = Victoria of Saxe-Coburg-Gotha

Boris (1877–1943)

Andrew (1879–1956)

Helen (1882–1957) = Prince Nicholas of Greece

Olga (1895–1918)　Tatiana (1897–1918)　Marie (1899–1918)　Anastasia (1901–18)　Alexis (1904–18)

Marina = Duke of Kent

Nicholas I
=
Alexandra
Feodorovna

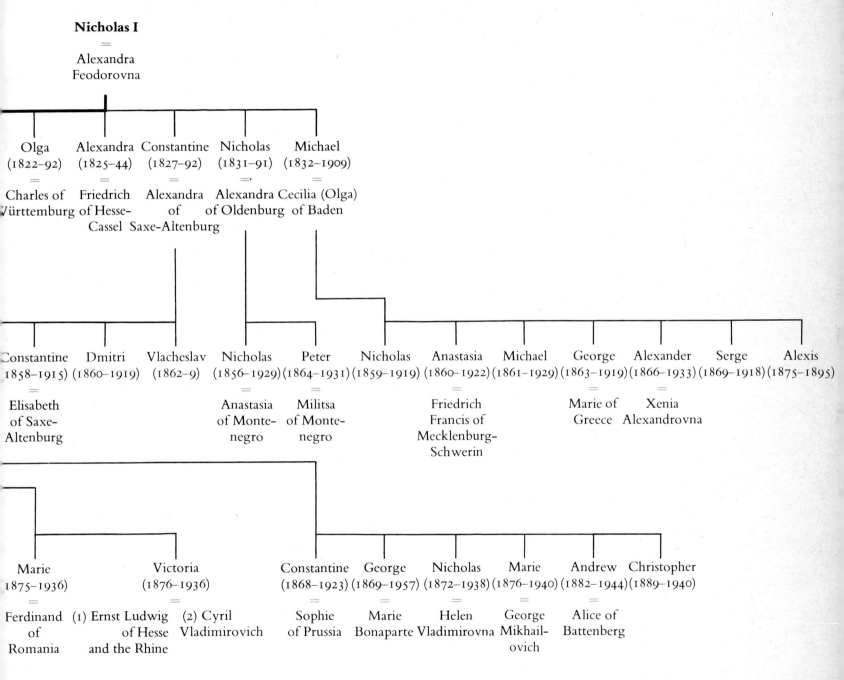

Olga
(1822–92)
=
Charles of
Württemburg

Alexandra
(1825–44)
=
Friedrich
of Hesse-
Cassel

Constantine
(1827–92)
=
Alexandra
of
Saxe-Altenburg

Nicholas
(1831–91)
=
Alexandra
of Oldenburg

Michael
(1832–1909)
=
Cecilia (Olga)
of Baden

Constantine
(1858–1915)
=
Elisabeth
of Saxe-
Altenburg

Dmitri
(1860–1919)

Vlacheslav
(1862–9)

Nicholas
(1856–1929)
=
Anastasia
of Monte-
negro

Peter
(1864–1931)
=
Militsa
of Monte-
negro

Nicholas
(1859–1919)

Anastasia
(1860–1922)
=
Friedrich
Francis of
Mecklenburg-
Schwerin

Michael
(1861–1929)

George
(1863–1919)
=
Marie of
Greece

Alexander
(1866–1933)
=
Xenia
Alexandrovna

Serge
(1869–1918)

Alexis
(1875–1895)

Marie
(1875–1936)
=
Ferdinand
of
Romania

Victoria
(1876–1936)
=
(1) Ernst Ludwig
of Hesse
and the Rhine

(2) Cyril
Vladimirovich

Constantine
(1868–1923)
=
Sophie
of Prussia

George
(1869–1957)
=
Marie
Bonaparte

Nicholas
(1872–1938)
=
Helen
Vladimirovna

Marie
(1876–1940)
=
George
Mikhail-
ovich

Andrew
(1882–1944)
=
Alice of
Battenberg

Christopher
(1889–1940)

Picture sources

We are grateful to the following for permission to reproduce photographs. The photographer's name, where known, is given in brackets. Unattributed photographs are from the author's collection.

General S. P. Andolenko: 83, 91–2, 113, 141, 221, 239, 246, 276, 301

Colonel Prince S. S. Belosselsky: 125–6, 128–9, 190–5, 196–8, 214 (Hahn), 244

Mme A. A. Benois-Tcherkessoff: 90

Mrs H. N. Bezak and P. Goudime: 28 (Levitski)

Colonel G. E. Bibikov: 280

Mrs M. P. von Bock: 47

Mme T. E. Botkin: 143, 275

Mrs M. Bowater: 220 (Neverovsky collection), 237

Captain Baron N. A. Dellingshausen: 176

Colonel G. A. Dolenga-Kovalevsky: 330

Princess Eugénie of Greece: 9, 11 and 13 (G. E. Hansen), 24 (Hansen & Weller), 27 (Levitski), 29–41, 42 (Fischer), 43 (J. Danielsen), 44, 46 (A. T. Collin), 49, 60–6, 68, 69 (H. Uyeno), 70 (Danielsen), 71 (Collin), 72, 73 (W. & D. Downey), 74, 75 (E. Uhlenhuth), 79, 89, 99, 100, 105, 108, 254–5, 283–4, 302, 304, 308, 311, 319, 321, 328–9, 334–5, 337–40, 343–4, 352, 354, 356

Archive of 4th Rifle Guards Regiment: 95, 120–2, 170

Pierre Gilliard: 135, 182–7, 199, 200, 215–16, 223, 226–32, 249, 273–4, 277–8, 281, 286–300, 303, 305, 307, 309–10, 312, 315–18, 320, 322, 324–7, 333, 336, 341–2, 345–8, 350–1

P. Goudime: 19, 20, 85 (Levitski), 112, 137, 165–9

V. B. Heroys: 45, 93 (B. Avanzo), 331 (K. K. Bulla)

Countess M. Heyden: 103

Colonel A. S. Hoerschelmann: 84 (Levitski)

Professor G. Katkov: 154 (Molokhovets collection)

Count W. P. Kleinmichel (album of Baroness Buxhoeveden): 313, 323, 355

F. G. Kozlianinov: 3 (Robillar)

T. N. Kulikovsky: 14 (Hansen), 15

Duke Serge von Leuchtenberg: 56 (de Jongh), 97, 117

Lieutenant M. G. Moukhanov: 147 (V. Otsupe), 258

Earl Mountbatten: (Prince and Princess Louis of Battenberg's album of 1883–1901) 57–8, (album of Miss N. Kerr) 106–7, 156–7, (Boissonnas & Eggler) 144–5, (album of Princess Louise of Battenberg) 148, 158–64, 175, (album of Baroness Buxhoeveden) 172, 177–80; 155, 205–13

Prince Peter of Greece and Nagaki & Co., Nagasaki: 67 (Nikoma)

Niva: 50 (woodcut of 1893), 81 (Demchinski), 82 (Semenov), 86–7 (General Nasvetevich), 110–11, 271

Mrs M. Merriweather Post: 138

Radio Times Hulton Picture Library: 55

Rosenborg Castle Royal collection: 6, 23, 96

Archives of St Petersburg Guards Regiment: 118, 201–4 (Lieutenant N. S. Palnikov)

Mrs Nina Spiridovitch: 181, 217 (Empress Alexandra), 218–19

A. Stacevich: 102, 146, 153, 247, 259

Baron C. N. Stackelberg: 263–9 (Empress Alexandra), 282, 285

A. B. Tatistcheff: 88

Lieutenant Baron G. N. Taube: 234

Mrs H. V. Tolstoy-Miloslavsky: 51

Mrs H. W. Torello: 59 and 94 (album of E. N. Kozlianinov), 260

Prince Vasili of Russia: 4, 5, 7, 8, 10, 12 (Levitski), 80, 115, 151, 233 (album of Countess A. V. Hendrikov), 272, 279, 332 (album of Countess Mengden), 349

Virginia Museum of Fine Arts: 1 and 21 (Levitski)

Prince Vladimir A. Romanov: 53–4 (de Jongh), 142 (Hahn)

N. N. Voeikoff: 22, 76–8, 235

Winter Palace collection: 2 (Levitski)

Photographers in the author's collection

Empress Alexandra: 270

K. K. Bulla: 109, 123–4, 130–4, 136, 139, 140, 150, 171, 188–9, 238

Hahn: 248

Levitski: 18, 25–6, 98

Timofeev: 257

Tsarevich Alexei: 306